THE
ELEMENTAL MOTORCYCLIST

Road Dog Publications was formed in 2010 as an imprint of Lost Classics Book Company and is dedicated to publishing the best in books on motorcycling for the thoughtful rider. This is Brent Allen's second book, which offers riding advice and his thoughts on riding in a conversational tone, rather than the dictatorial manner of so many "how to" books. These are not hard and fast rules of riding but gentle suggestions for riders to consider as they grow in their riding experience.

Riding a motorcycle involves a certain amount of inherent risk. Even when practising good motorcycling skills, accidents and injuries may occur. We take no responsibility for accidents or injuries while a rider is following guidelines as set out in this book. As always, the rider is exclusively responsible for his or her actions and should use common sense based on training and experience when riding.

The Elemental Motorcyclist
© January 2012, Brent Allen, All Rights Reserved.

ISBN 978-1-890623-38-8
Library of Congress Control Number: 2012933823

Road Dog
PUBLICATIONS

An Imprint of Lost Classics Book Company
Visit us at http://www.roaddogpub.com
This book also available in e-Book format at online booksellers. ISBN 978-1-890623-39-5

The

Elemental Motorcyclist

Brent Allen
aka
"Captain Crash"

Publisher
Lake Wales, Florida

About the Author

Brent "Crash" Allen grew up in the San Francisco Bay area, graduating high school in 1981, the same year he bought his first motorcycle—a 1978 Honda XL500S. Receiving his motorcycle endorsement that year, he has kept it current ever since.

Trained and certified as an Idaho State Motorcycle Safety Instructor in April 2003, "Crash" teaches both basic and advanced motorcycling classes. He was awarded the Shining Star award by Idaho STAR in 2004 and an Award of Merit in 2010.

"Captain Crash" is well-known in the motorcycling community, having produced the popular series of motorcycle safety videos titled "Howzit Done?" which have received over three-quarters of a million views on YouTube.

The author has owned sportbikes, standards, dual-sports, a motard, and now a cruiser. An equal opportunity rider—if it's got two wheels, he'll ride it.

Early on, Brent worked as a truck driver, equipment operator, light duty mechanic, pump jockey, and a freight handler. He attended college at Foothills College, Santa

Monica College, and eventually Brigham Young University, where he was awarded a bachelors in Mass Communications in 2011. Brent went to work in broadcasting in the Salt Lake City area in 1986. He moved to Idaho in 1990, where he worked as a television photojournalist, production and operations manager, and producer/director. Brent has worked on nationally broadcast football and rodeo events as a camera operator since 1986.

In 2002, Brent was hired as a Professional Technical Educator and now teaches broadcasting to high school students. In 2005 he was voted "Teacher of the Year" by his high school teaching peers. His students have been the SkillsUSA Idaho State Champions in Television (video) Production from 2005 through 2010, SkillsUSA National Champions in Television (video) Production in 2009, and SkillsUSA Idaho State Champions in Broadcast News in 2006 and 2009.

Brent is also Fire Commissioner for the Nampa Fire Protection District and is proud to be helping first responders do their jobs and do them well.

This is Brent's second book about motorcycling. The first, *Motorcycles, Life, and...*, was released in March of 2011.

Foreword

The Elements of
Motorcycling

This is not your mom's motorcycling manual. If you're looking for a solidly organized, insightful manual chock full of flowery prose, a heartfelt tale of the road hammering home helpful hints, or even just a dry "How To" book, then you've cracked the wrong cover. I will not be decoding the mystery of the countersteer for you. I find debating "center of gravity" and "coefficient of friction" dry if not boring. If you want a lot of cerebral discussion about deflection then consider yourself deflected—it ain't happening here. I have no calculations to share or epic theories with which to burden you.

I am not a scientist or a physicist. I am not a mathematician or mechanical engineer. I am not the guy you want to do your taxes or figure the tip—I just like to ride.

Oh, and I like to have a good time on a bike, too. I believe that God intended for us to have fun on bikes. I believe he looks the other way when we brutalize the speed limit and that he will not count it against us at the judgment bar. There is no time in purgatory for wheelies or stoppies. I believe that it's not just the Angel of Death that rides a bike; I believe the regular, good angels do too—because no one would take a job where they didn't let you ride. I believe that, yes, I have seen Jesus on the outside of that turn I came into a little hot. I don't believe he was there to shake his fist and smite me; I believe he was there to root for me and I also believe that may be how I got around that turn. I believe bikes are good.

I am no angel and I am no devil—I just like to ride. If we're out and you feel like I'm riding like an ass, rest assured I'm a happy ass.

I believe there are no bad bikes. There are good bikes and great bikes, and any bike is better than no bike. There are no bad bikes, just bad bike owners. Bad bike owners worry more about other people's rides than they do their own. All the silliness that folks parade out about "real bikes" or "man's bikes" and "squid" or "pirate" insults are simply posturing and you shouldn't let it bother you. If someone has time to spend calling you names then walk away and ride your bike; it is time better spent.

Bikes are made for riding and not riding your bike is a sin; it may color the way the Lord looks at your other, lesser sins.

There is a theory out there that "riding isn't for everyone"—that's true, it isn't. Some are physically unable to ride, some are mentally incapable. The problem isn't in telling the difference, the problem is in sharing the news. Let me be very careful here—the only person who really knows if you can or can't ride is you. Being honest with ourselves is about impossible when it comes to riding. We all spend a lot of time lying to ourselves about how well we ride, and conversely, how poorly we ride. Lies we also tell ourselves include things like, "I'm riding this bike at its potential," "This bike makes me look good," "I make this bike look good," and "What can you teach *me*? *I* already know how to ride."

We all have something we can learn. Even the most pedantic, confused, and muddled knucklehead has something he can teach you—if you'll just listen. Sometimes others' failures are well-crafted lessons to be learned.

There are some "safety advocates" whom I would like to walk up to, remove their helmets, gently cradle their unprotected cheeks in both my hands, and then head butt—knock them cross-eyed for a second. And there's a few "The Man ain't gonna make me wear a helmet" types I'd like to give the same treatment. Why? Because sometimes blind allegiance to an idea is more annoying than simply being wrong...it's the worst kind of wrong because it is wrong pretending to be right. My point: riding without a helmet doesn't guarantee you'll die or end up eating through a straw all your life. Riding with a helmet doesn't make you a sheep. If you don't want to wear one, don't. If you do wear one, great. It's your call. I believe in the old adage, "Whatever gets you off, just don't get any on me."

Stop splashing it on everyone, OK? Do your thing and stop waving your thing around like I care about it. No amount of demanding I care about your thing is gonna get me to.

This is a motorcycle book. It is not *the* motorcycle book. There are lots and lots and lots of motorcycle books and a couple that might be *the* book; but this is simply a book about how I ride and what works for me. Scripture? No. Sensual? Yes. That's why it's *The Elemental Motorcyclist,* not *Riding Basics* or *How to Ride.* This is about the feeling, the texture, the mindset, and the passions of riding. There are no calculations to read, no tables to scan, and no diagrams to dissect; we didn't even put one picture in to let you know what a good, hot, and sticky tire looks like...this is about riding from the body not the brain. I'm not going to parse words and get all wonky about terms; I'm just gonna talk about riding.

The essays in this book fall into four catagories: *Earth, Air, Fire,* and *Water,* because those are the elemental powers. If you're shaking a fist at me and saying "What about Ether?" then accept this: *You* are the Ether. I chose the four elements because to me they mirror steps or stages that we go through as motorcyclists. To me each phase mirrors what we go through in our journey as riders.

Deciding how to categorize things is difficult. You can use age, size, make, model, type, weight...you name it. Putting things into a pile and giving them names is not an easy business. Frankly, there are as many ways to sort as there are things to sort. During the writing of this book, I realized that there were fundamental categories motorcycling anecdotes fell into. I like the four primal forces: Earth, Air, Fire, and Water because, well, motorcycling is such a visceral, sensual thing that tying it to the basic forces of nature just makes sense.

EARTH

Often when you decide to ride you may feel you made an impulsive decision but if you really, honestly look back it's been there waiting like a fault line, with pressure building up, energy stored in a static state, waiting to be released. Not all riders take the same path to riding. Some are truly flights of fancy; you see, you buy. Some are the results of years of careful planning and meticulous preparation. But the bulk, it seems to me, are a combination of the two, a middle ground, a place where planning meets opportunity and someone suddenly says, "Yeah, let's go to Vegas and get hitched!" followed by a blur of roses, rings, and lingerie and waking up the next morning blurry eyed asking, "Did I really just do that?"

By no means do the Earth bits of the book follow or track those events; rather, the Earth essays offer insights into things that can, do, should, and maybe oughta happen during that ramping up to buying a bike. Oh, I know you're reading this saying, "No, I was walking down the street minding my own business, and this motorcycle jumped out and handcuffed itself to me! I had no choice, it was sudden and violent and wonderful and I never saw it coming!"

Liar.

The idea had been there like some quietly waiting, predatorial Krakatoa that you never, ever saw coming... Oh grow up; you knew it was there. You knew you wanted to act on it, you just had to wait for the right second and POW—*you* released Mount St. Helens and started killing trees and tourists. You may not have been expecting that hyperactive, superheated ash flow, but you knew something was coming. The hope of a slow moving lava flow patiently working its way to the sea, with you having lots of time to control things, is suddenly gone, and you're running from a guy who's waving a credit report saying, "You're totally qualified!" You know he's gonna get you.

Fast forward and you're sitting in the garage trying to figure out what to tell the significant other.

The Earth essays deal with the preparation you might hope to have and the groundwork you may or may not lay. Most importantly, they deal with the idea that you've really always wanted a bike, you consciously or unconsciously laid the groundwork, and somehow it finally happened. If you see yourself in these stories and topics, that's great; if you don't then that's OK too. I just hope you have a good time reading them.

AIR

What is the sound of Joy? Of unadulterated, childish happiness? What was the sound in your head when you finally, at long last, got to kiss that special someone?

I don't know either, but for my money it sure as hell sounds like a motorcycle. The Air essays are about that ethereal feeling of euphoria that owning your first bike brings. What color is happiness? Probably the color of your first ride, red in my case. As always these actually have subjects and issues that you can use to improve your riding, or you can just fondly remember your time in the heavens. If you find your experience doesn't match mine that's OK, too, because Baby, ain't none of us the exact same. As they say, "Your mileage may vary." These are the sunshine essays laced with Vitamin R(ide), good times and good to eat.

Enjoy. Have fun. Reminisce. Learn from the good times.

FIRE

I was a news shooter for the local ABC affiliate back in the day—I've seen fire. I've had a fire boss order me to retreat from in front of a forest fire, and I mean directly in the path of a big, crowning, running fire; standing there listening to that amazing sound of destruction as firefighters hotfooted it the other way to decide where to make a stand to try and save a cabin or decide if it was time to save themselves. The big man threatened me with real violence if I didn't leave. I've stood out on a soccer field shooting pictures of a burning building before realizing that the firemen were all hiding behind their trucks and I reevaluated my positioning. (They were waiting for the other propane tanks to explode.) I've been to house fires, trailer fires, restaurant fires, forest fires, and grass fires. If you've been around fire you realize the absolute destruction it brings. It has the ability to reduce a structure to a smoldering pile of carbon with nothing left but bedsprings and the shell of a stove—it's amazing and brutally destructive.

Being around fire means being around firefighters and I'm lucky, I'm now a fire commissioner. I get to help plan the course of a department, to cut the checks that release the funds that make patrons and firefighters safer, and most importantly, firefighters seem to like me. It could be an elaborate fake to make the political boss happy, but I like to think they like me.

Are the Fire essays full of stories and situations telling how dangerous riding is and all the terrible things that might happen? I don't believe they are. When I speak of fire and riding I'm not talking death by fire, I'm talking trial by fire—those things that may not only certainly endanger us, but also the things that test us. As you read the Fire pieces, don't see danger, see opportunity, the chance to learn from others, to live a little farther in the future, to be a better rider, and maybe a better person. Fire doesn't just destroy, it also refines.

WATER

Water gives birth to some of the truly wonderful, sexy, exciting motorcycle words; words like *flow, liquid, smooth, surge, fluid,* all great words that should make you think about those moments when you and the bike are like mercury squirting down the road, running around anything in the way, seeking the fastest, smoothest course. Water is beautiful in the way it won't be denied. You can block it, dam it, divert it, and being one of the elemental forces it won't give up its relentless search for the lowest point and the path of least resistance.

We live on a small farm (16 acres) and we flood irrigate. I'm here to tell you, water is a sneaky, determined rascal.

Water, once it cuts a path, really doesn't want to change; you have to be sure to create something that it can't break down or knock over; as the farmers say: "It's hard to run water uphill." You're better off to work with water than try to force it to do what it won't or can't do.

The Water essays are about the bits of riding that signal you've come to that place where you have internal flow, that your chi is serene, your personal Feng Shui is aligned; that basically you've got your shit together and can ride a bike. Consider this: after you've ridden long enough you reach a place where one of two things can happen—you become complacent or you become competent. The Water bits are about that place and the joys and dangers that live there. Loads of folks ask to know when they are "expert" or "accomplished." They worry about when they are credible or complete. Don't ask me, don't know. Still learning. However, every once in a while—hot damn, I can ride a bike! Those moments of liquid grace are hard to describe, almost impossible to predict, and beautiful in their own way. They are also the times when you find that centered place and...balance. It may be at 5 mph or 105, on a canyon run or grocery run, you might be on a long trip or just tripping to work, but somehow you get to that place where you're in the zone. Hard to explain—easy to catalog. Earth, Air, Fire, and Water; they are primal forces, and riding is a primal business.

Pretentious, maybe, but I like it, and I'm at peace with it. I hope these help you and that you enjoy them as well.

Be Safe.

TABLE OF CONTENTS

FIRST BIKE—PART ONE

When people ask me what their first bike should be I always want to answer, "A 250cc dirtbike when you were 14... maybe a 125cc when you were 12." In my opinion there is no better time to learn to ride than as a kid and no better place than in the dirt. Unfortunately, giving this advice to a 19, 29, 39, 49, 59, or 69 year-old doesn't do much good. Yes, those ages have all passed through training classes at which I have been an instructor.

So you are aware: Yes, I live in the real world, and I understand that not everybody gets a dirtbike at twelve or fourteen. And, no, I did not get a dirtbike when I was twelve or fourteen. I got my first bike at age eighteen; bought it myself. It wasn't a dirtbike, nor was it a street bike. It was a dual-sport bike. If you ask me what bike I recommend for a first bike for a nineteen-year-old I will say, "Dual-sport." The reason is simple—dual-sports are cheap, easy to pick up, easy to repair, and very forgiving to ride.

Your first bike shouldn't be a bike that punishes your rookie mistakes. Yes, I know that someone reading this is saying, "But I bought a XYZ1400, and it didn't kill me." To which I answer, "No, it didn't, but how much did it cost you when you dropped it at the gas station after you slipped on diesel at the pump?" See, your first bike isn't your last bike just like you didn't marry the first girl you ever dated. Your first bike is your *first* bike and subject to first rider errors, which is why you want a bike that won't punish a stupid mistake. How 'bout a quick list of rookie mistakes and how a first bike should mitigate them?

1. **Throttle Boo-Boos**—A first bike shouldn't punish a mistake on the throttle. That means that if a new rider accidentally wicks it wide open or turns it too hard the bike won't jump to attention, saying, "Sir, yes, Sir!" and then hoist the front wheel or suddenly be going 60 mph in a cul-de-sac or dead-end street. You want a bike that will pull your weight and get out of its own way, but not become a bucking bronco if you accidently give it the spurs. If you're a horse person let me put it this way: You want an older gelding who ain't gonna go until you make it perfectly clear that's what you want him to do.

2. **Braking Mishaps**—New riders often grab the brakes, and bikes don't like that. A front suspension likes to load up as you brake and that calls for a firm, progressive squeeze, the kind the pastor gives you when they're asking, "Where ya been, Crash? Long time, no see." Grabbing the brakes doesn't give time for the front to load, and that can lead to the front locking—which is survivable as long as you release the brakes and reapply properly. Any steering input while the front is locked is not going to end well. The larger and more sporting the bike is the more the brakes become wonderfully effective things that can be violently misused. You don't want a bike that under performs, but remember a high performance bike will have monster brakes and will not suffer fools lightly. You don't want bad brakes, but high performance ones can cost a lot of money and pain.

3. **Gravity Attacks**—Gravity works. Do the Newton. Hold an apple at arm's length and let go. The apple will fall

to earth...just a like a motorcycle you try to get off of before putting down the side stand. Yep, in my experience as an instructor one of the most common falls is when someone dismounts without having his or her side stand down. Had one happen just a week ago. The lady managed to catch the bike and hold it up until we got there to help—and that bike was a 330 lb., 250cc cruiser. Imagine what would happen with a 750 lb. bike or a nine hundred pounder. Yes, you can lift a bike that big back up, but the point is you're probably gonna have to let it fall, and falling could mean damage, and damage means money. Not to mention the fact that 800 pounds of bike on top of you can be a burning hot, bad idea...you want a bike that is small enough that you can manage it easily and manage a situation where gravity is on a rampage.

4. **Insurance**—Had you thought of that? Different bikes have different costs to insure. For a starter bike I like something you only need public liability and property damage to cover (maybe some medical, too). I'm a believer in the idea that first bikes are good for about one or two years, and then you can move up. Insurance-wise, on my first bike, I just carried the minimum because if it was so twisted that I couldn't fix it, it was done anyway. I didn't want to pay $1000 dollars in insurance to have them pay out $600. At that point in my life I'd have rather banked the money and spent it on gas and girls.

In essence what you're looking for is a user-friendly bike that won't pound you into the ground for making a mistake or cost you an arm and a leg if it needs some cosmetic touching up. That leads me to dual-sports, motorcycles that are basically dirtbikes with a headlight, brake light, and turn signals. *Please* remember: I'm not talking about your last bike, but your first. Odds are really good that you'll own several over the years. I was just talking to a fellow who's on bike seventeen. Me? I'm on nine or ten, but the idea is the same: you'll change bikes every once in a while. I like dual-sports because they are forgiving and cheap to fix, and you can fix them yourself. Are they the only bikes that make good starters? Absolutely not.

There are several 250cc bikes on the market that I think are spectacular first bikes, and most cost between three and four grand brand new. That can be a little spendy for a first bike so a trip to the classifieds or a cruise on the web might be in order.

I teach high school and about half my students are sophomores—that means fifteen-year-olds. I've noticed a strange phenomena that takes place when you're fifteen: you fall in love for the first time and apparently it's forever...or so it is to the fifteen-year-old mind. As you know, it is usually puppy love or infatuation, but to the fifteen-year-old mind he's "The One," "The "Only One," and and it is "Perfect." All this "only perfect one" leads to some excitement when it is "over."

When I was a young man, breaking up was a pretty simple business. You called her up (or she called you) and said things like, "Maybe we shouldn't go steady anymore," and she said, "Good point," and that was that. Nowadays, in this age of mass communications, you'd think a text would be enough—but no, it's not. Here's how it seems to play. You walk your girlfriend up to my classroom door and then stand around and small talk until just before the bell rings, and right when there's just enough time to haul your butt to Sophomore English you say, "It's over! We're through!" and you run like a bunny. Then the heartbroken fifteen-year-old girl comes into my room and starts crying, as I explain that radio was originally called "wireless telegraph" because all they could do was interrupt the signal, causing a click and enabling them to send Morse code.

Marconi and wireless communication shouldn't make you cry, so I have to ask, "What's wrong?" and her classmates say, "She just got dumped," and I say, "Take the tissues and go into the hall. Becky will take notes for you. Get it together and get back in here as quick as you can. If you can't pull it together go to the counselor's." There's a little pity party out in the hall, and eventually everyone comes back in.

In the next few days I end up mentioning that when you're fifteen you're not "in love," and "that dude ain't The One. Love struck teen girls don't like hearing that, especially when you turn to the little girl who was crying her eyes out two weeks earlier and you ask, "Who you dating now?" The answer is inevitably a different boy, to which I say, "I rest my case."

Your first bike isn't your last bike. I suggest that your first bike is a training bike, and you might own it for as little as six months to a year. That first date you have in high school isn't with a supermodel or twenty-seven-year-old architect, it's with another fifteen or sixteen-year-old because you're both still learning, you're going to make mistakes and have wonderful moments of discovery. In the motorcycle world you do the same thing. Look for a bike that is your equal—one you can grow into and then outgrow. There I said it. Get your first bike to be your first bike, then you can start looking for the second...and the third...and the fourth...

FIRST BIKE—PART TWO

One day, you're sitting in your car and decide that you want to be a motorcyclist. You take a course, pass, and get endorsed. Then you have to buy a bike, your first bike. How do you make that decision?

The amount of things you can do on a motorcycle is truly staggering. You can use them for work or play, at war or peace, and in most any kind of weather. Folks use bikes to go to the four corners of the earth or just to the corner bar. They deliver medicine to the impoverished and ill in third world countries, courier documents in large cities, or they just deliver smiles on the weekend. Some scooters have outstanding mileage, and others drink fuel like an overloaded SUV. Some have you lay on top of them like a missile, others you sit in like a recliner. Some have seating positions that would make a nun proud in Bible class. When it comes to motorcycles, you can find a bike that will do just about anything you want, a bike specialized to the task you have in mind. It hasn't always been that way. In 1981, when I bought my first, there wasn't near the diversification of motorcycles that you see today. We had dirtbikes, a few dual-sports, cruisers, and the "universal

Japanese motorcycle" (UJM), which was a pretty basic bike you could bend to do about anything you wanted it to do.

A note: I'm going to skip dirtbikes on this list—they are specialized machines for use exclusively off road. In this list we're talking road bikes; if I don't list your breed or sub-category of ride in the following list, see it as proof of the breadth and width of style and configuration. There's just sooo many different ways to parse riders and their rides that making a comprehensive list is probably impossible. That said, nowdays you'll find, and this is definitely an incomplete list, all sorts of things in your street motorcycle salad.

1.   Cruisers Oh my, are there different kinds of these, too! So you know, the vast majority of cruisers are V-twins, but there are some wonderful parallel twins, triples, and a couple of V-4s that are in this class.

    A.   The first major divide is American or metric. *American* means it's made, or assembled, in the United States. These bikes measure displacement in cubic inches. *Metric* means it's made somewhere else, and the displacement is usually measured in cubic centimeters (cc). Metric or American is probably the great divide in the cruiser world. Once you've established which it is then the true diversification begins.

       i.   Standard—This is the basic cruiser you see out there. Relaxed riding positions, feet under you or forward, it can carry two comfortably, and is pretty easy to spot as the most popular cruiser you'll see.

      ii.   Choppers—Raked out, long, often hardtail (no rear suspension), small gas tank, don't steer really well, look "da bomb." See any myriad of early 2000s Discovery Channel build offs to see them being created. Usually more art than transportation. Small fuel tanks, seats one, not always comfortably. Don't figure on wanting to carve the canyon or bust out 500 mile days.

iii. Bobber—Another classic look, generally short rear fender, front isn't stretched. Bike looks more like a standard cruiser that has been modified and stripped. Generally seats one fairly comfortably. Often with a small fuel tank and limited range.

iv. Dressers or Baggers (touring)—These are cruisers designed to get you over long distances comfortably. Look for large fairings and saddlebags. A large capacity fuel tank is important to these sorts of riders: they are going to do interstate travel and want to be able to go long distances and carry their stuff with them.

v. Muscle—This is a fairly new one. You'll find, now, that manufacturers are building high output versions of their cruisers. Specific selling points are things like quarter mile times, horsepower, and torque output. Bottom line? These are bikes designed to win stoplight drags. (If you don't know what a stoplight drag is or haven't been in one, sorry, I ain't gonna explain it, but it's probably what you think it is.)

2. **Sportbikes** These are usually four-cylinder inline bikes that are "race replicas" and have tremendous performance capabilities. A derogatory title for them is "crotch rockets" because of their speed and performance. Extraordinarily popular with young men, these bikes will punish a rider who gets in over his head. Turn the throttle and they will go, lay on the brakes and they will stop. Seating position is feet high and behind you, you lay over the tank, weight on your arms and wrists with low, narrow handlebars.

A. Naked Sportbikes—This is a subcategory I really like. These are slightly detuned sportbikes that are lacking the body work and have a more conventional seating position. They remind me of the universal Japanese motorcycles of the early 80s. These have the grunt to get out of their own way and have excellent brakes.

Nakeds are easy to make into sport touring bikes (more on those later).

B. Streetfighters—Once you throw a sportbike down on the ground, you'll find that buying all that plastic to put it back into sporting trim can cost a lot of dough. Riders found that if you don't put the bodywork back on, and add a new headlight and handlebars, you can end up with a road warrior bike that has all the performance of a race replica but the inexpensive street-tough look that makes for a unique bike. Several manufacturers are now building streetfighter-style bikes you can buy in the showroom.

3. **Standards** Feet under you, straight back, upright position, generally comfortable seating for two. Handlebars in the upright position. This was originally the turf of the "universal Japanese bike," just the standard motorcycle you'd have seen in the 70s and 80s. Honestly, there ain't many of this sort of bike around nowadays; the specialization of the market has made them scarce.

4. **Touring** Baggers and dressers are touring cruisers. They have cousins that are simply designed for interstate and long distance travel.

A. Straight Up Touring—These rides have copious storage, radios, GPS, and Bluetooth, rider/passenger communication systems. Built for riding long distances, they have large protective fairings and are designed for long turns in the saddle.

B. Sport Touring—Ever see a police motorcycle that wasn't a V-twin? Then you were probably looking at a sport tourer. Riders in this niche are looking for performance over comfort in their long distance travel. Often using a naked sportbike as a platform, these bikes are at home taking the long way and hustling down a canyon road.

C. Adventure Touring—Part dirtbike, part interstate touring rig, adventure touring bikes are designed to go anywhere. Say you're an actor and just wrapped shooting an important science fiction trilogy, and you're looking to blow off steam by riding across Europe...and the middle east...and India...and China. Then you're after an adventure touring rig. Huge fuel capacity, durability, and on or off road capability set these bikes apart. Often they appear to be dirtbikes' larger, hulking, brute cousins; they are designed to go absolutely anywhere—paved or not.

5. **Dual-Sports** These are dirtbikes with lights. Long travel suspension, light, usually single cylinder, and designed to do time on the trail, as well as Main Street. I believe these are outstanding rides to learn on: tip it over and it won't cost you much, light enough to pick up, and easy to work on and modify—if that's your thing. Some people put adventure touring in this category, but I believe that although there are some dual-sports that can be turned into nice touring rigs and adventure touring rigs tend to look like dualies on steroids, they are different animals.

    A. Supermotos—A subcategory of dual-sport is supermoto. These are dirtbikes with sportbike wheels and tires on them. They are glorious fun, and all I'll say is that I'm biased and love them and, yes, they make a great starter bike.

What does this all mean to you? It means that the odds you'll have one bike and stick with it forever are about zero. Why? Because bikes that fit all your needs are hard to find; the universal is pretty well gone. Back in the day you could buy one bike and then ride it, change the bars, add some bags, throw a fairing on and off...pretty much make it the bike you wanted... now the factory does that for you. The problem is what if your tastes change? Now the platform you start with is already finished—you can't really build it like you used to. Sure, you can add on, but the bottom line is bikes are so focused that all you're going to do is change colors and add farkles.

I'm saying there's a good chance that as your tastes and needs change, so will your motorcycle. Let me offer this sage, age old advice again: It's your first bike, not your last. Because you change, because bikes are so specialized, there is little chance you're going to hook into one bike and ride it forever. Oh, you may have one you never sell—that's my supermoto story—but you'll find that as you age you might not be able to crouch over a sportbike anymore. Or you might find that a chopper ain't the thing to drive to work every day. Could be you decide to ride that bike to visit Mom or the kids on the coast which means you need a bigger gas tank and some wind protection.

See what I mean?

Ultimate Responsibility

There is a school of thought out there that there are no unavoidable motorcycle accidents. Read this as: Whenever there is a motorcycle accident the motorcyclist failed in some way and carries responsibility for the wreck. How could this be? It's an intriguing idea called "failure to anticipate," which means basically, "you should have seen it coming." If a car suddenly merges into your lane and creams you, then you failed to anticipate that car's possible action, and by not creating a greater space cushion you're on the hook. As ideas go I love it and hate it.

I like the idea of ultimate responsibility, the idea that we are responsible for our own world, being aware of it around us and acting to create the best riding environment possible. In all frankness, we often try to foist the responsibility for our wrecks off onto something else. How many dozens of times have you read or heard a rider describe his or her accident like this:

"I was leaned over in a turn and there must have been some gravel or oil on the road, and the bike just went down..."

or

"I was following this cage and suddenly they jammed on

the brakes. I did everything I could and now my forks are bent..."

or

"I made eye contact with the driver, but he still turned into my path. There was nothing I could do and now I'm off the bike for at least six months."

In the ultimate responsibility world all three fall under the heading of "failure to anticipate." Rider one failed to anticipate a poor surface condition (though in reality he probably came in hot, got leaned to an uncomfortable angle, got on the brakes, spent all his traction, and lowsided). Rider two failed to anticipate a potential sudden stop by the car in front (which he was following too closely). Rider three failed to anticipate that eye contact doesn't mean the other user actually internalized "seeing" him and should have anticipated a potential right of way violation.

It's a brutal "it's all on you" philosophy, and part of me really, really likes it. It's probably the part of me that wants to pin a scarlet "A" on Hester Prynne. I kind of like knowing we have some control over the world around us and should own our mistakes and victories. It's a bit of a Puritan, no mercy, all-suffering kind of thing, but it has its advantages. First, you get to mentally and emotionally beat yourself up every time something goes wrong—but on the flip side, since everybody is in the same boat, you don't have to show sympathy or empathy. In a big picture way we all get what we have coming, so it's all on you, so screw you! I find that approach appeals to some dark part of my soul that likes to gloat and feel smart because "I wouldn't make that mistake," but it also leaves me feeling a touch cruel.

That "failure to anticipate" world is a tough one, because in the end it requires us all to properly anticipate *everything*. We have to guess all other users' intents correctly and adjust correctly; we have to be able to anticipate irrational and neglectful decisions by others. Weather, traffic, mechanical issues all have to be faithfully and correctly anticipated along with every possible problem. Is there anything wrong with expecting riders to anticipate? Absolutely not! But that pressure of correctly ferreting out all the possibilities can be a mind killer. You can end up so wrapped up in "he might," "they could," and "is that a" that you can't ride the motorcycle.

Mull these over and tell me how they feel.

1.   Bike gets rear-ended in traffic. It's the rider's fault because he failed to anticipate being rear-ended and had no escape plan. Sure, he flashed his brake light, but he shouldn't have been in the center lane where he had no escape—knucklehead.

2.   Biker is traveling in a rural environment. Traveling at 55 in a 55. On his right, as he approaches an intersection where cross traffic has a stop sign, he notices a car pull up and stop. The car waits according to the law. Biker continues on his way, and when he's about 50 feet short of the car, it surges out into the intersection (remember 55 mph is 75 feet per second). He strikes the car's driver's rear quarter panel and...he failed to anticipate a right-of-way violation so it's the rider's fault. He should have seen the car and slowed down...lots...allowed himself enough room and speed to get stopped—irresponsible rider.

3.   Biker is travelling across country. It's twilight and early spring. As he travels he is going down a two-lane state route, traveling at the 65 mph speed limit. A deer jumps from cover and lands immediately in his path of travel. Before he can brake, he hits the deer, tears it in half, loses control of his bike, and falls to the pavement. As we know, deer are more active at dusk and dawn...they startle easily...and he should have...ahhhh...errrr...anticipated deer in the area and adjusted speed to have time to brake or evade! (Wasn't sure I could get that one to be his fault there.)

Sometimes I prefer a bit more random world where bad things happen to good riders. Sure, riders might place themselves in a riskier position, but riding always carries risk with it. Risk and random bad luck are more than passing acquaintances. I'm not relieving riders of the responsibility for their actions or the consequences of their decisions. I'm simply saying that sometimes there are things a reasonable person can't anticipate. As riders, we are ultimately responsible for ourselves, but we also rely on a small modicum of other users behaving responsibly. When people ask me to define what an "accident" is, I have this pat answer:

"An accident is when two people do the wrong thing at the same time."

Example: We live on a small farm. We have 16 acres, and we keep cows, horses, chickens, a couple of goats, dogs, and cats. We have about eight acres in pasture and eight in hay. In the past we have cut, baled, and stacked our own hay. (We don't bale right now because I blew the baler up and can't find another one, but that's a different story.) Once you cut hay, it lays on the ground for few days to dry before you bale it. If it rains heavily on the hay you need to rake or turn it so it can fully dry out. One time we had the hay down and it rained pretty good. Mrs. Crash and I took an implement called a "Hay Fluffer," hooked it to the back of the tractor, and went out to "fluff" the hay. (I know what some of you are thinking and you're criminal perverts. Clean it up!) As we fluffed the hay (Stop it! It just lifts the hay up and sets it down so air can pass under it.) we found that the cut was really heavy, which is good news because it means lots of hay.

The fluffer would, on occasion, jam and stop working because of the amount of hay. To un-jam the fluffer you could do one of two things: stop, put the whole rig in neutral, and pull the hay out by hand; or if you caught it early enough, you could stop and back up a couple of feet. To set the stage, Mrs. Crash usually rides on the tractor with me, but on this occasion she was walking along next to the fluffer just keeping an eye on the mechanicals. If it became jammed, I could put the tractor in neutral, and she could step in and unclog it; or I could wave her back, put it in reverse, and back the jam out.

You know what's going to happen, right?

Of course, because when two people do the wrong thing at the same time you get an accident. The fluffer jammed, I put it in reverse to clear it, she stepped in to clear it, and when all was said and done the lovely and delightful Mrs. Crash got an ambulance ride to the hospital, a tib/fib fracture, a titanium rod in her leg, and an apologetic husband who still has nightmares of accidently killing the most important person in his life to this day. If I had looked? If she had waited to be waved in? If either of those two things had happened we wouldn't have had an accident, and a year or more of pain and rehab would have been avoided. Heck, a lifetime of explaining, "I didn't run her over—I backed over her," would have been avoided.

There are times when you're out on the road, and you have a momentary lapse and get away with it. Like just now. When I was riding home, suddenly there was a police car right on my six, and I have absolutely no idea where he came from. He wasn't there one moment, then big as life the next. I never saw him sitting on the side of the road or catching up to me; he just appeared behind me in some startling Houdini move. After shocking me by appearing—I'm looking around for the speed limit sign—when I look back he's gone! Like a ghost. That kind of crap happens...but it's also his job to be stealthy and to able to appear and disappear with magical precision; that is part of what cops do! Should I beat myself up for being surprised? A little, yeah. He had to come from somewhere, and clearly I had lost track of what was going on behind me; but in the long run I am only responsible for me. I should have seen him before he got the drop on me; but hey, it's his job to get the drop on me.

The place I'm trying to get to here is that when you're on the bike sometimes crap happens. At times it's your fault, other times it's a shared responsibility, and other times crap happens. I'm a guy who, when talking about ultimate responsibility, will not beat you about the head and shoulders and tell you that you failed to anticipate. Why? Because sometimes crap happens, and when you ride a bike you need to own that responsibility—the idea that you might get caught out, that things might go wrong, that in the end there is some stuff you just can't control or anticipate. Friend, as long as you're willing to say, "I ride, I do my best, and well...even then, who could have seen *that* coming? Shit can happen," I'm cool with that. I am not making excuses for sloppy riding or being asleep at the switch; I am saying it is OK to be human and let others be human, too. Nobody's perfect...well, one guy is, but he's cool about it.

Your Skillset

It turns out that the research says getting rider training is excellent help for your survival during your first six months to one year of riding. After that? Ahhhh...well, not so effective. In other words, a year after their training, trained and untrained riders have the same crash rate—there's not a large statistical difference. Why? First, like a medication, the effects of training appear to wear off. Skills are perishable. If you don't rehearse them, they fade. Does any of this mean you don't need to get trained to ride? No, to me it's pretty clear that if you're going to learn to ride that getting training is really important to your short term survival. At its heart, the real question is: What happens to riders that causes trained and untrained riders to merge into the same crash-prone bunch after a year? Do untrained riders suddenly become as good as trained riders, or is it something else?

Being old, cynical, and having worked in professional technical education, let me offer my unscientific opinions.

First, rider training gives you a perishable skill set that has a maximum lifespan of about one year.

Second, the School of Hard Knocks ain't a bad teacher; but she's no edumacation goddess either.

To the first point—I believe that the edge that beginning riders get from being trained slowly fades until a trained rider is (your choice) as good or as bad as an untrained rider. This being a totally unscientific paper and completely based on my anecdotal experience all I can say up front is: Bail out now if you want, because I got nothing to prove this except a feeling. The general riding public fixates on the idea of training as inoculation—once injected, training will last forever. I view it as booster shots which need to be regularly given. In the short ten years I've been in close contact with safety professionals, I've seen the development of multiple intermediate and advanced rider training courses. That says to me that the "establishment" understands that riders need to refresh and hone their skillset.

To the second point—the School of Hard Knocks will knock skills into you. You can't help but learn the rudimentary riding skills you need by riding on the street. However, that explains why the crash rate for those untrained riders is higher in that first year. It's not called the "School of Gently Imparted Facts." It's the School of Hard Knocks for a reason; skills get beat into you on occasion. I learned to ride at the School of Hard Knocks. I was on the pavement within my first six months. Call it the short course on "compromised road surface, traction management, and throttle control."

However you learn, skills will fade if they're not practiced. Ideas, strategies, and concepts shift deeper into memory and can be lost if they're not refreshed occasionally. Once you learn to play Mozart, you have to play it once in a while to keep it fresh in your mind and skillset. You physically and mentally need to practice to retain your skills.

When I'm helping a high school student learn a complex piece of editing software, I adhere to a classic educational philosophy: repetition builds retention. If you've taken a training course, you'll remember that during that training you did exercises which are designed to help you repeat certain behaviors over and over and over in order to drive them into what's called "muscle memory." You're embedding stuff into your brain so it becomes automatic. As you're trained you may or may not notice that something that is learned in one exercise is repeated in the next. You get information that is layered, and you build on it. In the very first exercise you're trained to "keep your head and eyes up"—that never goes away. I'll be coaching in the last exercise of a training cycle and I'll still be saying "eyes up" to people on the range. It's something that is in the curriculum to be coached all the way through. It is a foundational skill that is reinforced through regular repetition. We are expected to train you to keep those eyes up, and we watch for it and help you keep them up by watching for when you start looking at your hands or the ground.

The concept of layering information, of laying a foundation and then building on it, and reinforcing old information while introducing new is very sound educational philosophy. Start with the basics, then build.

The problem for riders can come when they neglect the foundation. I get a lot of questions from people about how to corner. They're worried about line selections, apexing, and body positioning, not to mention trail braking or weight bias or countersteering. The two most important things I can say to them are, "Where are you looking?" followed by, "Are you countersteering?" Nine out of ten times the issue isn't the line or where your body is, it's about where you're looking and if you are able to actively steer the bike. Looking and steering are also foundational skills that can slip. Training, even one session every couple of years, will keep those foundational skills honed.

You got knives in your kitchen, don't you? Are they sharp? Who sharpens them? How often? Or do you just do what lots of folks do, and when the current knife is dull you just pitch it and hit the box store for some more? Admit it, you've thrown dull knives away because you don't want to screw around sharpening them—you have some disposable knives in the kitchen right now, I bet; ones with plastic handles right? Around Hacienda de la Crash, we have disposable knives and then other knives that we sharpen. For the record, we keep wooden handled knives, and plastic is for throw-aways.

In your toolbox of riding skills are a bunch of knives. They are not disposable, but they will simply get dull if you don't use them. You know that phrase *hone your skills*? Honing a knife means resharpening it regularly to keep its edge. Yeah, you *sharpen* knives when they're dull, but you *hone* them regularly so they don't become dull—so they don't lose their edge. Riders need to hone their skills.

How can you hone your skills? As the infomercial says, "It's so easy, you won't even know you're doing it!" Remember, you *sharpen* things when they are dull; you *hone* things to keep them consistently sharp.

Keeping the idea of honing in mind, every time you ride you need to be aware you are riding. By being alert and aware, scanning and cataloging, and thinking about what you're doing; you're honing your mental skills. You will find there are times you are riding on auto-pilot; that just happens—especially on roads you ride every day—so you need to be aware that you're not focused on the job at hand and keep your mind on task. Mentally I drift, you drift, we all drift; but the issue is to come back on task, and once back on task, to stay there. Every single time you ride you can be honing your mental skills. I'm often shocked by how easy it is to slide in behind a car, truck, or even another rider and then shut your brain off and simply follow whatever is in front of you. I still find myself riding comatose sometimes...but remember that keeping your mind active and engaged is the first step to keeping your skills honed.

Physical skills need honing as well. I believe that advanced rider training can be used to sharpen or to hone. Riders should be aware that we get rusty, and getting rid of rust could require sharpening, and, friends, sharpening is grinding so you reshape the metal, cut away the imperfections, and create a new cutting face. Once that new face is created, you hone it to keep it sharp. For the experienced rider a refresher course is an excellent way to make sure your cutting edge is cleaned up. Having a professional watch you ride and point out problem areas is a blessing you don't want to miss out on. Complacency about your skill set can lead you to think your knife is sharp, when in fact it's as dull as a donut. As a rider people often try and convince me that I've "got it going on," which I don't. I'm lucky, because I get to go to "Professional Development Workshops" and train a couple of times a year and get feedback from professionals who are willing to look hard at my riding. I expect to be coached. I expect to have weaknesses pointed out. I know I can be better, and I feel cheated if someone doesn't give me honest feedback.

A good mindset will also save you from the pains of attempting to be perfect. You want to be perfect in effort, but perfection in execution every dang time is a weight you don't want to be packing. I work to perfect my technique and understand that occasionally I'll clip that cone or go a little longer than I'd like on a stop.

Chefs have an old saying: "A dull knife is more dangerous than a sharp one." Why? Because you have to work so much harder to make a dull knife cut that you lose control of it. Rather than cut, a dull knife compresses and then tears—it will suddenly start moving and is difficult to finesse. I hone my skills whenever I can, and professional help makes it a finer edge.

Practicing in a parking lot can help you hone your skills individually, as well. How often you ask? How about 15 to 30 minutes a week? I'm not talking about sharpening. I'm talking about honing. Ever see a chef pick up a knife and give it a couple of swipes with a sharpener?—honing. That scene from your favorite western where the hero gets a shave usually starts with the barber giving his razor a couple of swipes on the razor strop to keep it honed. All you need is a few free minutes on the way home, and you can pop into that empty church or school lot, run it up to 25, and practice your emergency braking, or slow it down and practice U-turns and swerves. You don't need to carry cones with you, but a real serious "throw some cones" kind of session wouldn't hurt in keeping a clean edge.

Can I tell you a ranch story? Here on the farm/ranch we feed alfalfa to our stock. We cut, bale, and stack it here on the property. Each bale is bound with twine. When it comes time to feed, you need to cut the twine so you can feed the stock the hay. A sharp knife is a wonderful thing to have when you're cutting bales open. A dull knife is an annoyance because you have to saw the twine instead of just cutting it with one stroke.

Here's a ranch secret: If you don't have a knife with you, you can cut twine with twine. Basic physics plays a big role. What you do is take a length of twine, pass it under the twine on the bale, then grab each end, and as you pull up, you saw it back and forth in long strokes. The twine on twine friction will melt the twine of the bale because you're working one spot on the bale and the twine in your hands is working twelve inches of space. This will get the job done and is to my mind easier than using a dull knife. Why? Because you're doing just about the same thing with the twine as you are with a dull knife, and the twine is easier to hold onto! What's the point? The point is that no matter how you came by it, if your skill set is dull it often seems easier to shortcut it and ignore it all together. If you're not good at U-turns and avoid them, no big deal; but if you're braking skills are crap and you suddenly need them, you'll regret having twine in your pocket instead of a good sharp blade. Hone your skills, and if you don't know where you're sharp or dull, get some training. It'll help. I will say this: I learned more in eight hours in an MSF class than I did in twelve months at the School of Hard Knocks.

The Religion of Safety

Sounds odd, yes? The Religion of Safety. I call it that because in some ways, when we talk of safety, we talk about it the same way we do religion. There are adherents. There are priests, popes, and apostates. Folks dabble in safety. They go through waves of fervency, sometimes becoming hardcore, other times lapsing.

I come from a religious tradition that eschews—make that forbids—alcohol, tobacco, and coffee. Use of these things is seen as moral failing. If you use them you are weak. There is no "upside" to them. If you're an adherent and fall into smoking—or even just have a beer once in a while—you're viewed as a failure. It's a weakness issue; you either can or you can't. There's no gray space for personal struggle or mediation. You are either in or you're out.

We tend to think of motorcycle safety in the same terms; either you're "All The Gear, All The Time" (ATGATT) or you're...well...apostate. We have terms that have popped up that highlight this disparity. *Squid* and *safety nazi* are good examples of derogatory names that are used to describe people and their perceived positions on safety.

I have been asked, "Are you a safety nazi?" *and* I have been asked, "Are you some kind of squid?" Sometimes when the safety-minded ask, it feels like, "Are you pro-adultery?" When the less-safety-minded ask, it can feel like, "Are you cool or uptight?" Being asked if I'm one or the other makes me happy. I worked in television news as a videographer and more than once I heard a news director say, "If both sides of the story are mad at you, you're probably telling it right." Yup. If the Democrats were saying you've got it wrong and Republicans agreed, you were telling the whole story—everybody's ox got gored.

Speaking of safety, we tend to only see the two positions; safety nazi or squid. Either you are safe or you are not. If you're not ATGATT then you're probably riding around in a wife beater T-shirt, flip flops, a backwards baseball cap, and sunglasses. Yet, when you look around you'll see this is patently untrue. If it were true there would be only two kinds of riders on the road—squids in their T-shirts and safety nazis in full gear; life on the other hand is a spectrum.

I make safety videos and wear a camouflage jacket. Guess what happens? Yes, I get nasty comments and e-mails about how irresponsible that camouflage jacket is. The fact that it's a dedicated, designed motorcycle jacket with armor in it doesn't matter. Somehow I've gone to the "other side" by not wearing a day-glow lime green with 233 square inches of retro-reflective material. To some, I'm "safety minded" but not orthodox enough. Here's where the real rub comes in. Say you've come across a young rider who's wearing a helmet, gloves, long sleeves, long pants, and a decent pair of boots. What do you do?

Often we shoot the hostage by jumping on them about getting an armored jacket *and* riding pants *and* you really should have dedicated riding boots. We don't look for the good things someone's doing. We look for the good things people aren't doing.

Does that make sense?

For me the clarity of the situation comes from personal religious experience and cultural issues with a cigar or a beer. Just like in motorcycling, religious folks often don't worry about whether or not the person drinking shares their religious beliefs or restrictions. The orthodox can often simply project their own personal beliefs and structure onto others. By this I mean, they look at someone who's having a smoke and rather than saying, "That fellow has a belief system that apparently allows smoking," they will look and say, "That fellow is a smoker. He shouldn't. That's a sign of moral failing." I say, no, he's not a moral weakling, he may or may not have the smoking monkey on his back. He may or may not be breaking his own rules. Who the flip knows? It's not my department. Yet, it's easy to look at him and say, "Addicted loser," especially if you're not a smoker. We don't see a spectrum of behaviors, we simply see our own black and white world; either you're in or you're out.

Unfortunately, it can be the same when we deal with other riders about safety. They are either in or out. You'll know when you've run into someone who's had his chops busted by the "safety orthodox" because he has a special name for those who forcefully evangelize safety; where did you think the term "safety nazi" with all its brutal baggage comes from? That nasty term comes for experience. From having someone walk up to you at the rest stop or the restaurant and bust your chops. Nobody is really looking for that knock on the door and someone asking, "Do you want me to tell you how you should live your life?"

If you want to talk to someone about safety issues, you need to stop and think a moment about how to approach it.

True story: I attended a major university that was sponsored by a major religion. At twenty-three I moved into the dorms. Why? Because food was easy to get, tasted good, and magically, clean sheets would appear every Monday. In Crash World that's three squares and a cot, and that's OK by me. The down side was that every Sunday morning some well-intentioned eighteen or nineteen-year-old knucklehead would knock on my door and say, "We're on the way to church. You coming?"

To which I would respond, "Save me a space, I'm running late," and then go back to sleep. These through-the-door conversations took place every week. It wasn't offensive. (Kids trying to help me "do the right thing" were well-intentioned.) No one ever opened the door or refused to go away; they simply knocked, asked, and then left. That I can respect. Nobody ever offered to wait or to help me shave or tried to force the issue. They simply let me know they cared about me, and then they hit the road.

Do you see how wrong that could have gone?

Knock, knock.

Crash: (mumbling) "Wha...Who? Yeah?"

Knucklehead: "If you don't go to church you're gonna burn in hell!"

Crash: "Hello?"

Knucklehead: "Yep, you're an apostate and your immortal soul is in jeopardy, Satan is trying to get his hand up your soul and turn you into his sock puppet."

Crash: "What?!"

Knucklehead: "You don't want to be Satan's sock puppet, do you? Of course not. I'm gonna recite the Lord's Prayer and the Ten Commandants out here until you put that tie on and come to church!"

You'd kill yourself. No questions asked. You'd climb out the window in your skivvies and run down the quad looking for a weapon. Yet, when it comes to talking about motorcycling safety, we have the same kinds of things happening:

Knock, knock.

Crash: "Howdy."

Well-Intentioned Other Rider (WIOR): "Hey, I noticed you're not wearing dedicated motorcycling pants."

Crash: "Well...no...but they are heavy-duty, double front canvas."

WIOR: "You should really wear something designed for riding. You should have some Kevlar and armor in there somewhere. Studies show that cotton explodes on impact—just BOOM and it's you and the asphalt grinding along in some sickening, flesh-melting lambada."

Crash: "Seriously. We're having this conversation?"

WIOR: "That's the problem with guys like you—you only go half way—what kind of example is that? Would you like to see some gory post abrasion pictures? I carry a few right here in my pocket just for these occasions. One is of a really pretty girl who can't wear swimsuits anymore. Got another with a guy who had ankle bones ground off...Are those boots purpose-designed for riding? You're really not very bright, are you?"

Crash: "Dude. Stop humping my leg. It may be fun for you, but I'm gonna beat you to death with my Snell/DOT/CE approved helmet if you don't knock this crap off."

See what I mean? If I'm lacking a piece of gear, why bust my chops? Why use an anvil to kill a fly? I'm nine-tenths of the way there already! A quick, "Hey, have you considered riding pants? Dude, there's some really nice ones made by Brand X that look good, fit good, got some abrasion resistant crap in there..."

See the diff? We shouldn't treat people who make other choices, informed or not, like they are especially dense children. That's demeaning and offensive. Think about it! "Hi, I've noticed you're a little dense and don't have a DOT approved helmet—I'll use small words to help you understand this..."

Another time we can get annoying is after someone crashes. Folks just can't resist the "I told you so" or "You're pretty dang lucky—next time you might not be so lucky..." comments. There's some kind of "A-HA! Gotcha!" that happens and we want to rub salt in the wounds.

'Nother true story from college at a religious school: One night after returning from an evening of Bible study at around two a.m., I did what most people do after a long night of Bible study—I hit the urinal. Imagine my surprise to find someone else in the communal bathroom. It's two a.m. Saturday night (or Sunday morning, whatever's your pleasure) and down the row a couple of privacy dividers is a decent eighteen-year-old, moderately religious kid.

He starts making noises. Whimpering, grind your teeth, bear down, and suffer through it noises; the kind of sounds that require me to ask, "Dude, are you alright?" To which he replies, "It just burns sooo bad when I pee. I mean I held it all day 'cause it hurts and I think waiting was worse."

Now, if you're like me and went to school in California in the 70s, by the eighth grade you knew that a painful burning sensation while urinating can only mean one thing, and that is a trip to the clinic. Having all the health classes that the state of California requires, standing there trying to put my own equipment back in the locker, I began my diagnosis.

Crash: "Do you have any discharge?"

Burns to Pee: "What?"

Crash: "You got any puss or stuff like that oozing out?"

Burns to Pee: "Heck no."

This is where things get tricky. I'm at a religious school. I'm standing not too close to a guy who's either in the early stages of gonorrhea or has chlamydia...so, what's my next move? Well, let's take a page from the old "My friend has crashed, will I help them learn and improve from this experience?" book. I could try:

"The Lord has put a pox upon your peepee because you have not been living the law of chastity. Hopefully you will repent of your sins and change your wicked ways. God clearly hates you and your wiener and all the places it has been. I hope you learned a lesson. Sinner. Good day, Sir. Unless you want me to tell you about how the clap and the Lord will make your peepee rot off...I have some pictures I carry just for these sorts of occasions if you'd like to see."

Can you imagine? Now re-imagine it with the idea that you want to render aid, not gloat; that you're looking at the situation as a friend looking to help, not hurt.

Crash: "Dude. You've got a girlfriend, yes? And you've been...off the chastity wagon?"

Burns to Pee: "Yes. Yes, we have."

Crash: "Well, either way you've probably given it to her or she gave it to you. The problem is this ain't gonna just go away, and her symptoms are harder to spot...You love her and all that jazz?"

Burns: "Yeah."

Crash: "Then you owe it to her to tell her. Here's what I suggest: Go to the free clinic in town. Both ya'll get tested—this ain't a fault thing this is a *fix it* thing. If she wants pastoral counseling, you go with her. You wanna keep fooling around? Then ask for birth control at the clinic—because the clap you can fix—being a daddy is forever."

Which set into motion a chain of events that resulted in two healthy people leaving the clinic and a tempestuous, modestly dysfunctional relationship ending, as so many college romances do, by parting company without any children.

The culture of safety needs to be shared. We need more riders wearing more gear, getting better training, and riding safer and smarter. Mocking them, trying to "scare them straight," or browbeating them isn't going to get you very far. Why? Because if all you care about is spreading the message, or being the hero who is spreading the message, or getting people to act like you do because you know better, then you're not going to get people to change. People change because they realize it's good for them to change, that someone cares and wants the best for them—not because you scared or bullied them. When I'm in a tight spot and a friend points out a problem then offers a solution, I'll listen. I'll listen to a friend over a preacher any day of the week. Teacher axiom: They don't care what you know until they know how much you care. Don't worry about how much you know—worry about how much you care and then act like you really do.

Too Old to Start?
Too Old to Stay?

Ever hear the old story—The Lady or The Tiger? You know, after committing some justifiable offense in Conan the Barbarianland you're caught, unethically convicted, and then after a few days of gruel with maggots, you're in a pit surrounded by drunks wearing dead animals and the only way out is choosing between two doors. Behind one is a Lady (presumably beautiful) and behind the other is the Tiger (presumably hungry, angry, and ready to feast). That's not where I am right here—in the Lady and the Tiger choice you at least have a shot at getting something good out of it. But how do you answer the ol' "Too Old" question? I'm not seeing a "lady" anywhere in this equation—all I see is pain and discomfort. I could insult a lot of people and make a lot of enemies if I'm not careful. One thing none of us want to admit is that there are a far too many rings in the trunk to pull off that nose grind or, hell, a quick 100 yard dash! So how do we admit to being in the position of not trying or ceasing to try?

I've jumped out of an airplane...for fun. I paid to do it. It was fun. Before I did it, I stopped thinking about jumping out of a plane and concentrated on the individual actions I had to take and do them well.

Here goes:

You can be too old to start riding; you just can. What is that age? I don't know; it is personal. No, that isn't a cop out. The issue is that we're all different—too old for me is different than too old for you. Am I too old to play professional baseball? Yes. Yes, I am, but I'm not too old to be healthy and have fun playing in an over-forty league. (I don't, I just picked baseball because I was thinking about a certain professional athlete that came to baseball a little too late...) The tricky part of this math is that the toughest parts of riding are really mental; things like situational awareness, anticipating other's actions, modeling the future, and doing risk/reward calculations are all done in your head, and age will give you an advantage in calculating and weighing the things around you.

But age also deteriorates response times, vision wanes, hearing declines, stamina drops. So somewhere in the decline of the body and the maturity of the mind comes a point where—well—you're not the shizz anymore. Some sayings are "truisms." They just say it and don't have hidden meanings. "Age and treachery will always defeat youth and strength" is a famous trusim because it's simply true. A crafty pro will always beat a young novice. Heck, I teach high school and occasionally a young man will offer that he could "take" me if he wanted. I always say, "No you can't. I fight dirty." To which they say, "So do I!" My response: "I've forgotten more dirty than you've ever learned...and if we're fighting, you're worried about style and I'm worried about hurting you as badly and as quickly as I can." Generally they say things like, "Oh...hadn't looked at it that way."

Age brings wisdom. Age brings experience. But at some point age and experience can't overcome the damage done to reflex and strength. Where is that? I do not know. But if you're considering starting to ride then you should. Here's my help for you. Ask yourself this: If you had to fight an eighteen-year-old, would you? Seriously! Would you fight, flee, or surrender? I ask because if you really think about mixing it up with a good sized teen you're really thinking about survivability—your ability to survive—and consequence—how much damage can you sustain and then recover. This isn't some cold war "mutually assured destruction" issue. This is "I need to be able to absorb some punishment and then heal back up again." It's a risk/reward calculation. Can you be crafty enough on the bike that the debt of your now declining speed and strength are fully compensated? And if, *if,* you fail and fall can you afford and endure the healing process?

I'm not putting any numbers on the board here. All I'm saying is that if you're sixty years young, can you get out into the fray and out-think the traffic so you don't have to out-react it? God forbid if you end up on the ground, can you accept the roadrash? Or the broken bones? Those are your questions to answer. One of the things I like about rider training is that it gives people a chance to test the water before committing. I would suggest that if you're an older person and thinking about riding that you take a class so you'll actually ride a motorcycle and have a chance to decide if it's for you. I've had people over sixty in classes I've taught; they are great, motivated learners. But they sometimes bring an interesting issue to the table with them: fear.

Fear is a strange, strange thing and hard to talk about. Culturally we read the word *fear* as weakness, cowardice, or a deficiency; fear is a moral failing or a failing of character. I think that's wrong. Fear is many things and one of the things that it can be is respect. Riders of a certain age bring a healthy respect of injury and healing with them when they roll into your beginner motorcycling class. I'm not quite fifty and I have a well-grounded respect for injury. If I get thrown down hard, I worry that I'll tear and all the sawdust will come spilling out...and have to be stuffed back in as well! I'm not particularly interested in getting hurt, nor am I obsessed with avoiding injury, but right before I tear off a wheelie there's a little voice that says, "Cover the rear brake—you bin this and you could be crippled up a long time."

Because of that personal calculation I don't wheelie as much anymore.

If you're not as young as you once were and becoming risk-adverse, you might want to try before you buy; give it a shot and have some grounds for your decisions. Fear isn't always a bad thing. Fear is nature's way of saying, "Be careful, watch out." Fear can be a reasonable response to increased risk. The issue isn't "are you afraid?" It's whether or not that fear is paralyzing or inhibits your ability to ride. Part of riding is expanding your abilities and boundaries; you have to start small (low risk) and then step up as you expand your skillset and explore different environments. Part of the challenge for those late to riding is building an adequate base skillset as quickly as possible. As you build that skillset, you need to be able to push your personal boundaries and be comfortable stretching yourself—you may not have the luxury of taking your time to slowly build a skillset. You may need to progress fairly rapidly. Are you comfortable doing that?

The question of being too old to start is, actually, exactly the same one you should ask when you're worried about being too old to ride; it is a twist on the old saying: "Expert riders use their expert judgment to avoid using their expert skills." Reverse that idea—turn it around and honestly ask, "Can my expert skills still save me if my expert judgment fails?" Yeah, if you end up in a bind can you get yourself out? I'm talking about the kind of honest self-inspection that is difficult to do. Honest evaluation of who we are and what we can do is not one of those things we as a culture excel at.

If you fall into trouble can you get yourself out? Or have your skills deteriorated? Are you quick to react? Can you modulate the brake well, or are you gettin' grabby in your old age? Worse yet—are you riding frightened? Are you committing a chunk of your processing power to the simple act of worry? Instead of planning an out, are you pondering the pain? Are you nervous? Are you thinking more and more about what your life insurance and will look like, or who is designated to make medical decisions if you're...incapacitated? Then maybe your subconscious is trying to tell you something.

Mature riders coming to the sport have an even more complex calculation to make. They have to ask themselves those other tough questions: "How long will it take a newbie like me to build up a set of expert skills? And once I have it when does it start to fade? Can I keep an edge for a good long time? Or, even, at all?"

Worse yet—what are the objective measures to figure out when you're starting to slip? Let me know when you have a good answer because I have no freaking idea. What's that test gonna look like? Give me a standard or measure, a "do this in that time," an "objective" test—there ain't one. This is a serious personal issue that can only be answered by a mature person using reasoned self-assessment and evaluation.

Bottom line? And you probably won't like this—they (insert faceless bureaucracy here) *they* ain't ever gonna take that license from you...not until you get so feeble you can't lick the stamp or read to check the appropriate boxes. *They* ain't gonna make you stop riding; that's a decision for *you*. Yeah, trust me. Take a look around in your own family; somebody's driving who scares the crap out of you—Aunt Nellie or Uncle Vern. They're 105 and somehow they get into that Olds 88 and plow down the road sure they're "safe," until they blindly park on top of a newsstand or drive through a sporting goods store. For us, for riders, the choice to quit might be even harder. I don't know; I'm not there yet. I just hope that when I'm there, I'll be mature enough to realize it and gracefully walk away before I hurt myself or someone else.

TRAINING

So, one day, you are in your car and you look up and ZOOooooooommmm, a motorcycle zips by. As you watch the chrome twinkle and fade you look out over the hood of your non-denominational crud coated car and think to yourself, "I want to do that." Which slowly becomes, "I can do that. I mean, really, how hard can that be? It's really just a big bicycle, right?"

PRESTO-DIGITALIS! You've decided to become a motorcyclist. Later, after dinner and a relaxing beverage, you decide it's time to tell your—(circle one please) wife, husband, girlfriend, boyfriend, companion, longtime companion, passed-out roomie, stray cat that snuck in the window, Jay Leno (*he'll* understand!)—that you're gonna get a bike.

"Not on your life!" spits a finger waggling stray. "But I'll take a class!" says you (wondering how a pizza thieving tabby became your "In Case of Emergency" contact).

"What are *they* gonna teach you?" says the stray, as it rifles through your empty pizza boxes and all those Jack-in-the-Box wax papers you've nibbled a little past the wax to get all the cheese.

Good question! What are *they* going to teach you? Allow me to illuminate.

The *vast* majority of training in the US uses the Motorcycle Safety Foundation curriculum. The beginner's course is called the "Basic Rider Course" and usually starts on Friday night with a classroom component, continues Saturday with range (on bike) training for four hours, four more hours of classroom, then completes on Sunday with four hours of riding and a short classroom session. Times vary from state to state and from provider to provider, so don't be surprised if it's a little different. As always, there's a test at the end—two in fact: a Knowledge Evaluation and a Skill Evaluation.

For many, during the evaluations is where the fear and confusion start. Allow me to disallow you of some illusions by addressing some common misconceptions about *any* sound motorcycle curriculum.

1.   The beginner instruction is *not* designed to get you a license. It just isn't. It's designed to teach you sound fundamental operation of a motorcycle. On point, beginner training is designed to:

   A.   Teach that motorcycling is a risky business—and *you* manage that risk;

   B.   Teach you basic operations: starting, shifting, braking, cornering, and swerving;

   C.   Teach you basic street strategies: things like "See and be Seen," lane positioning, space cushions, traction issues, SEE (Search, Evaluate, Execute);

   D.   Allow you to practice riding and do emergency maneuvers in a controlled environment.

2.   The curriculum *is* designed for complete newcomers. It just is. The design is so you actually learn how to *sit* on a bike. This is ground-up, first-time, never-done-it-before training. You will find people in your course who might have some level of experience, but a beginner course is designed with utter, total, complete rookies in mind. You do *not* need any prior coaching, private lessons, or riding experience to

be successful in the formal training. The only thing you need to do before your course is any pre-reading that your course supplier sends to you or directs you to.

3. You do *not* need to buy gear or anything special to take beginner training. You've probably got what you need in your closet.

    A. Long sleeved shirt or coat

    B. Long pants (over the ankle...no capris!)

    C. Over the finger gloves—A pair of leather work gloves will do.

    D. Sturdy, over the ankle shoes—Some will let you go with a pair of leather hightops. The best?—maybe a lightweight hiking boot. If you're not sure, bring them with you to your first classroom session and *ask*. (Better to find out Friday night than Saturday morning.)

    E. Eye protection—Sunglasses are usually acceptable.

One question you'll hear a lot is, "Do I need a helmet?" Quick answer: *No*. Every place I've ever seen or heard about has "loaner" helmets they will let you use. Don't be upset if they ask you to wear a hair net when you use it. They're not worried about you—it's the last person that wore it they're worried about.

4. Chow—You will be given breaks. Bring something to eat. Yeah, it's only four hours on a bike, but that's gonna be six to ten miles of riding in potentially hot or cold weather. Bring snacks and a sports drink if you want one. The course provider will have water on hand but not much else. Like riding, you take a lot of responsibility for yourself. In my case, as an insulin dependant diabetic, I make sure *I* have everything *I* need: insulin, snacks, hydration, glucose monitor—you're going for a long motorcycle ride in a small parking lot—might as well treat it like what it is.

5. Passing or failing the course—Here's the tough one. What does passing *really* mean? What does failing *really* mean?

Passing means—you performed well on the evaluation! You did it. You proved some proficiency at operating a motorcycle. Many states have decided that passing the Motorcycle Safety Foundation: Basic Rider Course (MSF:BRC) evaluations (both Knowledge Evaluation and Skills Evaluation) is good enough to waive a state *skills* evaluation. You will probably still need to take the state's *written* examination. This is where some of the confusion starts for this *whole* adventure. The MSF:BRC isn't designed to get you a waiver—it's designed to equip you with basic skills and strategy. The Skill and Knowledge Evaluations test is to see if you *retained* those skills. States, seeing you've retained those skills and that knowledge (retained them for about, what? An hour?), often waive their skills test.

Yeah, passing means you're a parking lot devil. You've *not* been in traffic. You've *not* traveled more than 25 mph, and you're *not* ready for that big cross country adventure. You're ready to ride around in a parking lot where everyone goes the same direction...You *do* have a basic skillset to build on, a firm foundation to launch a motorcycling career on. You're off to a good start.

What does *failing* mean? It could mean many things. It could mean you had a bad day. It could mean you panicked during the evaluation (better on the range than the road). It could mean you need more practice. Failing does not mean you're a bad person.

Failing does not mean you're a loser.

Failing does not mean you can't learn to ride.

What failing means is that you may need another whack at the apple. You *can* retake the course. You can look for one-on-one instruction. Heck, you might even realize that you're a passenger, not a driver. Most importantly, failing the course means you need to get inside your own head and figure out what you really want to do—then chase it.

A word of caution in all this: If you're taking training from someone who guarantees you'll get your license, get out. It's in their interest to lie to you—to tell you that you're ready when you're not. Would you want a doctor cutting on you who had gone to a school that guaranteed everyone who entered would graduate? Me neither.

Everyone learns to ride for their own reasons. True story: Last year I was giving a lady the good news that she had passed the skills evaluation. I asked her, "What next, getting your license?" She answered, "No, I was looking at a list of things I had written down; a list of things I was going to do before I was 40. Learning to ride a motorcycle was one of them. My 40th is next week. Now, I've learned to ride! Thanks!"

Nice lady. Good day.

I thought about calling this "*Your* Emotional Needs" but decided against it. There are three basic emotional/coaching expectations you *should* have when you start a beginner's course.

1.   You are a person. You deserve respect.—You shouldn't be yelled at, belittled, or called names. You *will* be spoken to in a loud voice—yeah, you're wearing a helmet, there are running motorcycles around, traffic may be passing nearby, and instructors need to speak in a loud voice so they can be heard. Don't freak out because an instructor speaks loudly. (Heck there may be a hearing-impaired rider in your class.) That said, they shouldn't be calling you "worthless and weak" and telling you to drop and give them twenty.

2.   Individual attention and support—Yep, they're supposed to be paying attention to what your doing. Like Santa, they are watching and should see if you're naughty or nice. They *should* be telling you, "Good Job," or, "Get your eyes up," and they can't do that if they don't watch you. Behind those wraparound sunglasses they are paying attention.

3.   Honest, *clear* feedback—If you're having trouble you should know it. If you don't, someone should tell you in *no uncertain terms*. A bad habit formed in training is a bad habit that might kill you later. Coaching should be clear, concise, and on-point. If you don't understand, ask a question.

Here are three common problems that you should avoid.

1. Don't be *needy*. There are up to twenty-three other people in the classroom with you and as many as eleven on the range at the same time. If you expect the coach/instructor to spend his or her entire day running alongside your bike saying, "You can dooooooo it!" you're wrong. A coach or instructor is responsible for watching *every* rider *every* time as they go by or perform an exercise. They will watch you. They will give you feedback, but they can't get into a long discussion about motorcycle rake and trail during a braking exercise they have twenty-five minutes to complete. You should stay on task as well. Some questions should be saved for a break. Oh, and trust yourself a little. If you're really screwing it up, they'll tell you.

2. Don't feel entitled. You paid your money, you got your ride; that doesn't mean you get an automatic pass. You may *not* be a rider. You *may* need more saddle time. If you don't get it, let the coaches help. Each exercise builds on the last so there's time to re-mediate problems later in the show. If you don't feel like you've got that "eyes up while braking" thing down tight in the first braking exercise, don't worry there'll be another *and* you can practice "eyes up" during the cornering exercise. Didn't pass the class at the end of course? That's OK—would you rather be lied to and sent out on the road with a killing habit or missing a key skill? Sorry, but riding's not for everyone.

3. Be responsible for yourself. Own it. The instructors cannot ride your motorcycle for you. If you're not there yet, focus. Be patient. Stay out of your own head. Ask, "How am I doing?" When you get the answer, believe it. If a rider coach says, "You're coming along—remember to keep your eyes up," then *keep your eyes up*. Do *not* let that into your head as "You suck." You don't. You just need to keep your eyes up. A coach will pat the bottom of their chin to remind you to get your eyes up. If they do give you coaching *accept* it; it's not a insult. Take the coaching to heart and listen. If you fail, don't blame

the coaches but *do* take ownership. Figure out where things went wrong. Oh, and don't hog the day demanding to be told where you're having trouble. Ask during a break or stay after and talk about it. Coaches *do* want you to succeed; they will try to help.

Finally, a beginner doesn't deserve to pass just because he or she took a course and paid the fee. Some of us just aren't riders. It's more technical than some can handle. There's too much information to process well for others. Some just find out they don't like to ride. Bottom line: Learning is just that— *learning*, a voyage of discovery. Some discover they are riders. Some discover they are passengers. Others discover they can do something they didn't think they could.

I hope you enjoy your journey. Start it right with some formal training!

GEAR

Why is it that every time I start one of these things I'm always ready to apologize for those well meaning folks who browbeat others about "how to do it right"? You know the kind that walk up and tell you how much "you're gonna regret not having a _____ designed specifically for motorcycle riding."

Here is my statement of belief concerning gear. You should wear:

1. A helmet—I prefer full face. Your tastes may differ but have something that protects the back of your head a little. Striking the back of your head on the ground is a common fatal injury with riders. When you get to heaven you can ask Indian Larry about that. Helmet manufacturers are making some cool looking stuff now, and if you look you might find something you like. Half is better than nothing so I'd take that as a reasonable thing to do. If you're not a helmet guy, that's OK, too, as long as you're honest and admit they are lifesavers but you'd prefer not to wear one. Honesty makes you a man in my world, and I'll not debate someone who knows the facts and still makes a

different choice than I do. Do what you gotta do, but own it.

2. Gloves—Everyone (well, most) will put out their hands to "arrest a fall," which means when we see the pavement coming we deploy the landing gear. Gloves give you abrasion protection when you fall and *if* you fall you'll want them.

3. Boots—Do they need to be motorcycle specific? Naw, but I'd recommend a boot designed for riding. The reason is simple—you're riding and a purpose-build boot will probably be more useful, comfortable, and designed for protection in the case of a fall. I like boots with snap closures (no laces to get caught on things) and good over the ankle protection. In the last few years manufacturers have started producing some very nice boots at reasonable costs. The new wave in boots isn't race boots, but boots designed for the recreational rider. You should check them out. When I was young I rode in pair of roping boots and those worked great. The issue is that now you can get a low priced, purpose-built boot for less—take advantage of the situation.

4. Long pants—Sounds obvious, but it's not; when the temperature rises people start shedding clothes and pants quickly become short pants. My advice? Watch a bicycle race sometime and see what those guys are wearing and how that works out for them. Bicycle racing involves extreme gear calculation as they trade abrasion protection for weight, freedom of movement, and climate control. They get to wear those groovy spandex pants—when they fall they get raspberries. Last night I was at the "Twilight Criterion" bicycle race in downtown Boise, Idaho, and man, were there a couple of wrecks! Those guys just went skittering across the pavement and into the curb. There appeared to be at least one broken collarbone, and there was enough road rash to make the place look like a hamburger factory. For my money?—long pants. Dedicated riding jeans work for me, lots of companies make reinforced jeans just for riding that will give you protection from abrasion and still look good. You can buy armored pants if you want. I have a pair of armored undershorts—hip, thigh,

and tailbone—that I wear when I know I'm going to get all stupid. My two cents? I suggest something between you and the pavement and the sand, gravel, and dog poop in case you fall—a barrier layer to at least take the first impact and couple of seconds of grinding. Skin isn't my first choice for first contact with asphalt.

5. Long sleeved shirt or jacket—Summer starts and clothes come off. You see T-shirts and muscle shirts and even the brave and bare-chested. (Ladies never go bare-chested, but I guess there are all those laws and frankly it would just lead to a massive pile-up either from interest or repulsion.) I wear an armored jacket at all times. It gives impact and abrasion protection which are things I might need in a tight spot. During the summer I wear a mesh jacket for airflow and comfort. I believe that going short sleeved on your bike does a couple of things that put you in a potential tight spot; first there's no protection in the case of a fall and second, you're exposed to sunburn, windburn, and dehydration. Long sleeves will help keep you protected from the sun and slow water loss. I have seen people fall on the training range at 20 mph in long sleeves and come up unscathed—anything is better than skin.

Are you a loser or an idiot if you don't wear all the gear I do? Absolutely not! Riding is a personal adventure everybody is in for different reasons, and everyone rides a different style. If you ask me, "Should I wear a vest?" I'll answer, "If you want to. You might look at armored vests, there's some out there now with some built in back protection and that would be cool."

Riding is in the long run a gamble. You can ride your whole career and never wear a helmet or armored jacket and never need one—it's the one time you need one and don't have it that things get all sloppy ugly.

True story: I was a Boy Scout and one year when I was fifteen I went on a fifty mile hike up in the boonies of the Sierras. At the time I was a Second Class Scout (and still am today) but was a decent outdoorsman. We were hiking at altitudes of about 7,500-10,000 feet and even managed to get to 15,000 feet on a one day expedition. It was summer but still got strikingly cold overnight, especially backpacking with lightweight gear.

Occasionally we'd come across these pastoral mountain meadows and, well, how do I say this? They were sometimes a trap. See, they weren't always meadows because sometimes they were marshes. Being good Boy Scouts we had two guides with us and one was very, very good at cutting across country to shorten the hike or get more territory in. One time we were standing at the edge of this big, big meadow and he said, "We can go around *or* we can cut off about a mile by crossing this." This, to my teenaged mind, was a fine and brilliant idea; a quick vote showed we all were in agreement, and we stepped out into that meadow.

Immediately, we sank a little into the bog. We began to learn the terrain and managed to figure out where the high spots were and stay a little dryer and things were progressing nicely...until we were really committed and it wouldn't make sense to turn back...because then the mosquitoes arrived. *Arrived* is the wrong word; they sprung, they attacked, they shock-and-awed us. It was amazing because there were so many and they were so damn big! Several had tail numbers and I think ticks were flying them; it was an insect vampire massacre. There was only one thing to do: We ran like hell across that bog, tripping, splashing, using other scouts for traction. We beat feet across that thing. When we got to the tree line on the other side, as soon as we were in the shade, the mosquitoes simply vanished. Having survived the hideous onslaught, we counted noses and hatched a plan.

We figured that we should rest after getting some distance between us and the bloodsuckers just in case they had some strange insect plan to let us get in the shade, drop our gear and relax before sending in the second wave. Being young and strong, once we got going we kept going. Walking through the trees one guide led while the other the guide worked his way up and down the line of guys, kind of looking us over and chatting us up. After an hour or so, as he walked along, he suddenly asked in a loud voice, "Jimmy, where's your sleeping bag?" Sleeping bags are attached to the outside of the pack, usually at the very bottom or the very top. We all stopped.

Jimmy's sleeping bag was gone.

Next was a stupid question that had to be asked. In his command imperative voice the guide asked, "Has anyone seen Jimmy's sleeping bag?" About four different variations of "No" floated up. Next was a quick inventory by everyone to make sure no other sleeping bags or other gear was gone. All were accounted for.

"When," asked the guide, "was the last time anyone remembers seeing Jimmy's sleeping bag?"

A dutiful scout replied, "It was there before we crossed the meadoooo...wow."

We were now a couple of miles from the meadow. The sleeping bag was probably somewhere in the meadow, and there was no guarantee we could find it if we went back. Going back meant losing time and potentially scrubbing one leg of the trip or making us miss our return to camp date, and if we couldn't find it then, returning for it would be a wasted trip. An executive decision was made. Cross country guide would take Jimmy, bushwhack it to a road, get help, get Jimmy back to Scout Camp, and then rendezvous with us later that evening.

Jimmy wasn't thrilled. In fact he was really upset and this is when he uttered some immortal words, words that stick with me to this day, words that when you're desperate to do something and you have the wrong tool but still want in, these words will stick with you. Jimmy said:

"But I have a space blanket!"

This was perhaps the saddest, funniest, most earnest thing I had ever heard a human being say at that point in my life and still holds a place in the top three. The beauty of it was that he didn't want to quit and was looking for anything to stay on the hike, and the hopeful excuse of a space blanket wasn't enough to keep him on. Trouble had found him and he was trying to wish his way around it. Potentially he would have survived with that space blanket, but it would be ugly, ugly, ugly and we'd have ended up babying him through the experience and possibly ruining it for everyone. What happened to Jimmy is the same thing that can happen to us as riders—once the trouble comes, we want to wish the situation better. Once you're at 9,000 feet and you've got no bedroll, you can try to fix it, but nothing works as well as that sleeping bag you don't have.

I'm not here to tell you that death is imminent because you're not wearing gear. I'm not going to show you pictures of maimed people and say, "They wish they had." All I'm gonna say is this: If you're ever in the situation where you need a piece of gear and you don't have it, that's gonna hurt and I feel for you my friend. Too bad you didn't have at least a space blanket with you; think about what you're wearing and why you're wearing it—I can't fault anyone who makes an informed decision whether it's the same one I'd make or not.

HYPERTHERMIA

An important skill is (believe it or not) keeping cool in the summer! That's right, it seems simple but we often forget that *Hyper*thermia is a serious problem for riders.

What is hyperthermia? From our friends at www.medicinenet.com:

> *Hyperthermia is overheating of the body. The word is made up of "hyper" (high) + "thermia" from the Greek word "thermes" (heat). Hyperthermia is literally high heat. There are a variety of heat-related illnesses, including heat stroke and heat exhaustion. Other heat-related health problems include heat cramps, heat rash and sunburn."*
> *http://www.medicinenet.com/hyperthermia/article.htm*

Basically, it means you start getting cooked. Fundamentally your body cools itself by sweating—it's evaporative cooling. The problem for riders is, if you start sweating you're steaming water out of the system. If you don't pour water into the system then you run out of water in your body, your blood will literally thicken, and then bad, bad things can happen to you. So you know: On a bike, you'll wick away the sweat—that gives you that pleasant cooling sensation—*but* you may not realize *you are sweating* and you *need to sweat* to stay cool.

Do you see the double edged sword here? Riding cools you but also dehydrates you faster. You can end up with *heat stroke*. Again from our friends at Medicinenet:

> *"What are the symptoms of heat stroke? Warning signs of heat stroke vary but may include:*
> *an extremely high body temperature (above 104°F)*
> *red, hot, and moist or dry skin (no sweating)*
> *rapid, strong pulse*
> *throbbing headache*
> *dizziness*
> *nausea*
> *confusion*
> *seizures*
> *unconsciousness"*

Note symptom number two—*no sweating.* That's the sign that the system is failing and you're in trouble. Do you see the conundrum? Ride to be cool, but in essence you're speed drying yourself. (Why the rapid pulse and headache? I'm told it is because your blood is thickening and is harder to move).

Another big problem is the fact that *confusion* is a symptom. Yeah, you get stupid or, as we say in motorcycle world, *impaired*. You start thinking, "I don't feel good...Maybe that double bacon, green chili burrito was a bad idea...I'll ride *faster*, get home *sooner*, and get some Pepto going..." instead of recognizing you've got a serious problem. How serious? IV fluids serious. Kidney or liver shut down serious.

You *can* ride in hot weather. Mrs. Crash and I just completed two, 280 mile days riding in 90 to 100 degree temps. How? By staying hydrated. A couple of rules to live by if you're riding in the heat:

1. Understand you're in danger. Simply "toughing it out" isn't an option. Just like the realization that the only cars on the road at 3:30 a.m. on a Saturday morning are people going to bad jobs, cops, and drunks should heighten your awareness;

you should say—it's gonna be *hot* and plan accordingly. Riding on a 97 degree day *is not* the same as riding on an 78 degree one.

2. Act like you're in danger. Stop hourly. Re-hydrate. Yeah, you may not be thirsty but get twelve or sixteen ounces of water down you at each stop. *Force* yourself. Remember: one of the symptoms of heat stroke is nausea. *If* you see hot and sick? *You are hot and sick.* Stop often and hydrate. Drink a low sugar sports drink every couple stops. You wouldn't set out across Nevada without a full tank of gas—keep your internal radiator topped off.

3. Wear some gear but remember what's going on. Mesh is nice but remember, that cooling breeze is also a *drying* breeze. If you're wearing vented gear—same deal. Gear will help with *sunburn* as it protects you from UVs. It will also slow evaporation, but you don't want to cook in your gear. Use the vents. And if you're riding in a T-shirt and vest, you're bleeding water, so act like it. (See suggestion 2).

4. Wear sunscreen. On your face. Under your chin. On the back of your neck. The reflected energy off the road (or your shiny bike) can blister you as well as the direct energy of the sun.

5. Use cooling aids—like a water soaked bandanna on the back of your neck; notice how quickly it dries and remember that's what is happening to *you*. I've used gel filled cooling rags and really like them. They cover the back of your neck and cool at the same time. Also, once they stop offering comfort, it's a good sign to stop and reload.

6. Know when the teeth of the day is. When is it hottest? I've always found 4 to 6 p.m. to be where the real heat is. Consider parking it up during the hottest hours.

7. Are you taking pee breaks? When was the last time you urinated? Yea, a full bladder means you have H_2O to spare—once you notice, "I haven't peed all day," you've noticed a key indicator that your body no longer has a reservoir of water. It's all going out through your pores and

not your bladder. You should be drinking *and* peeing.

Remember, over heating is a serious and dangerous problem. It impairs you. An impaired person makes bad decisions.

The single most important thing you can do is: solve the problem before it becomes a problem. Be proactive, not reactive. Hydrate. Cover up as much as you can. Stay out of the teeth of the heat. Be wise.

HYPOTHERMIA

*Hypo*thermia is the opposite of the *hyper*thermia. Hyper =
too much. Hypo = too little. Hyperthermia is when your body
is too warm; hypothermia is when your body is too cold. Since
you're reading this and this is a book about riding, I will assume
you are a motorcycle rider, and as such, may well have had a
bout of either, whether you knew it or not.

Hypothermia is when your core body temperature drops to
a dangerously low level. Your body then no longer functions
as well as it should. Your body, to conserve heat, will shrink
its capillaries, forcing blood back to your body core in order
to attempt to keep your organs warm. Truly, it is crazy; your
body literally tries to pull itself into the center, sucking your
blood in, willing to let your extremities freeze to save your
core. Think of it as evolutionary triage where your body
decides what it can afford to lose.

With the way the economy has been the last few years
this shouldn't be a novel idea to riders. Sometimes you let
something you value go in order to save something that is
vital. You might sell the second bike or buy used instead of
new. Those getting divorces have felt the pain of having to

decide what to lop off. The trick of it is that when the lawyer or the court officer or the bookkeeper is on the phone it is really easy to understand you're in a bind. Red ink is red ink and we all can read it and know that something's gotta change—downsizing is coming—the hatchet is gonna fall—cutbacks are cut-outs.

When your body does its survival thing and starts pulling that bonus blood flow back to your core, guess what happens to your brain. Yeah, you become impaired; you get stupid. Professionals tell me you should watch out for the "umbles"—stumble, mumble, fumble, and bumble. The tricky part of this whole thing is the same problem you have when you're having a few beers: you may not realize you're in real trouble until you've passed a point of know return. I use "*know* return" because there's a point out there that, once you're past it, you *know* you're not getting back. Odds are you've done this with gas on your bike more than once. You know how far you can go on a tank and once you get beyond halfway you know you need to get more fuel or you're not making it back.

If you drink you know that out there, somewhere, on the continuum of wasted, there's a point where there's a big sign written in your own language and in your own hand that says, "You're really f*cked up." When you get there you know it, and usually you back off. The problem with hypothermia (or hyperthermia for that matter) is that when you see that sign—when you realize that you can't get the key out of, or into the ignition—you might not recognize that you're pretty fouled up—enough so to potentially need professional medical attention.

The key is to not start down the road. To carry the metaphor forward it means: don't start drinking and you don't need to worry about getting drunk. In matters of staying warm you might want to avoid riding in cold weather. Yup, think about wind chill for a moment. All that cooling that the movement of riding does during the summer is converted to wind chill in the winter. A quick check of the National Weather Service shows that at 40 degrees with a 35 mph wind equals a wind chill of 28 degrees. Speed that wind up to 60 mph and the wind chill is 25 degrees. Great galloping Jimmy Olsen that's pretty cold, especially if you're going to be going 65 or 75 miles per hour. If your plan is to be a human popsicle then you're well on your way.

This should not be construed to mean that you can't ride in the winter. I often do. It means that if you're going to do any foolhardy thing you should be cautious about how you do it. Rules of thumb:

1.   I won't ride if it's consistently below freezing because I like ice in my soda, not on my roads. If the temperature has not been above freezing for a few days then ice might not have been able to melt in shady or sheltered places. To my mind hitting ice just ain't worth the risk. I don't mind cold but I need a dry cold.

2.   Water makes things worse. Cold is one thing, cold and wet is a whole lot worse. I don't mind being a little wet in the spring or summer, but once there's a bite in the air I don't want to be wet because it amplifies the effects of the cold. Yeah, remember how you soaked your shirt in the summer to help with evaporative cooling? Now that's working against you. You're never more miserable than when you're wet and cold.

3.   Layer up. I start with a warm undergarment, then layer on from there. If you start with lots of layers you can always shed them if you're too hot. I will often top off with my rain gear for two reasons; first, it is a windproof barrier layer and second, it is bright yellow with retro-reflective stripes which increases visibility when other users might not be looking for motorcycles.

4.   Know when to quit. The best time is before you start, but if you are out on the road, stop and reheat yourself as often as possible. Remember to strip out of your gear and let it warm back up to room temperature. Look for chemical warming pads if you need to. Keep your wits about you, and don't press yourself; it's better to be late than never.

5.   Electric gear is a good thing as well, just remember that it's usually limited to vests and chaps. Electric hand grip heaters are also great. (We use them on the ATVs around the farm.) One thing to remember—don't get a false sense of security—if you're wearing an electric vest, your core's nice and warm, but your feet and hands can be at risk. Being aware of your overall condition is vital.

No, when I was a kid I did not ride to school in the snow, uphill both ways. I turned eighteen in the San Francisco Bay Area, and a bike was my only transportation for a couple years. It wasn't that bad in the Bay, but a long ride on a 35 degree morning still sucked. Now I live where the temperature overnight can hit -15 degrees in the hardest parts of winter. I might spend eight to twelve weeks off the bike, and that means that in my desperation to ride I'll head out when the high for the day is gonna be 35—sometimes you just gotta ride. Those rides are short, around the block, down to the deli kinds of things. Yes, I know someone reading this is calling me "sissy" and mumbling about those 300 mile days in North Dakota in December and, friends, that's great but for me, color me pink not blue—call me a fair weather rider but most importantly call me a guy who hasn't been bit by Mr. Freeze and I like it that way.

Parking

Got nerve? Got a bike that will jump a curb and easily fit in that blank, empty space between the ice box and the newspaper dispensers? I do. And yes, when I'm out on my 300 lb., 400cc, long travel suspension supermoto I'll jump the curb and park in strange places...because I can...and usually I'm not going to be there very long, so I figure I can buy a half dozen sunflower bagels and get out of town before the parking enforcement officer can get there. Go ahead, hate me; I don't mind. If you can pull off that fantasy parking job then you might as well go for it, but remember you can get a ticket for parking in stupid places. Parking laws were created to keep parking chaos under control. First responders need clear pathways to approach businesses, and customers need to get in and out of those same businesses. Because commerce requires access there are some questions you should ask yourself before freelancing a parking spot next to the door of your favorite deli.

1. If you are a regular then you should ask. Yeah, park out with the civies in the lot but don't be afraid to ask, "Do you mind if?" You'd be surprised how often the manager will

say, "Sure, if you're not blocking anything." Or you might get, "Do that, and I'll have you towed." In the long run, it's better to ask and find out before you start parking large. Mom was straight-up right: being polite and asking is the best way to proceed, especially if you're looking at a parking place somewhere you frequent. That means at work as well—you might even ask the boss to come look at the place you want to park and the pathway to get there. My boss doesn't mind me riding a hundred feet up the sidewalk to park in a sheltered corner. This I know because I asked.

2. One-offs. A one-off means that you're somewhere you're not a regular at—you're running into a bait shop on the way to the lake. (What? Never seen fishing poles strapped to a motorcycle?) You just need to run in and grab something. Then maybe this is a time to grab that small gap between the dumpster and the corner of the building and stuff your bike into it. I cannot tell you to park illegally because I don't know what constitutes illegal parking in your town. But I can say this: If it ain't clearly marked as no parking, if you're not impeding foot or vehicle traffic, then you have a decision to make. Good luck with that, just remember that if you're on private property, like a market or restaurant, your biggest concern is not annoying the property owner.

What helps me is having a couple rules of thumb, a couple basic guidelines to follow. Here are mine.

First: Am I blocking anything? And I mean anything at all. Does anyone have to walk around my bike? Does it block a walking path or access to the outdoor restroom? Does it block any signs or advertising? Simply having to throw a hip out to avoid a turn signal makes it a nuisance, and property owners hate nuisances. If you're not parking in a marked parking spot you risk a ticket or a tow—the first step in the wrong direction is getting noticed. You get noticed by putting your bike someplace where people go, "That thing's a pain."

Second: Is there anyone I can ask? Do you know what a "Cart Cowboy" is? It's the teenager who rounds up the carts in the parking lot. If I'm thinking about putting the bike up in an out of the way space near the front of a privately owned building (read *store*) I will park it and ask a Cart Cowboy, "Is this OK here for a few minutes?" If Jimmy pauses and says, "Maybe," he could be saying his boss is a weasel, and he's not sure how big a weasel the boss is. If he says, "Sure!" then he's willing to take the heat for it, which probably means he's not worried about the boss freaking out.

Third: Is it expressly forbidden or even implied that you shouldn't park there. Yup, striped islands at the end of a row of parking stalls vividly infer that nobody should park there. That doesn't mean that I haven't parked there, but that striping sure says, "Do not park here," and if I have a problem because I parked there I got no right to piss and moan about it. If there's anything that in any way says "NO" then think about it seriously. That striping may be part of the perceived space for handicap access or for a fire lane, so use your wits. Best bet is to leave it alone. Likewise, with parking near a door or fire exit, a big blank wall with one door is tempting but that door could be a fire exit so think it through, are you blocking egress from the building or can people freely get out in case of an emergency?

Finally: At public buildings, meaning buildings owned by the state or municipality, park in the marked stalls. Never freelance it. Try putting it on the sidewalk at the DMV and see how that works out for you. Simply put, the city or state can get you cited quickly and easily. Don't mess.

When using a marked parking stall I like to make sure I'm pointed nose out when I park. Usually, I accomplish this by pulling through an empty spot and into the one I want to use; that's just the bar-none easiest way to get it done. I do not like paddling backwards out of a spot into a busy lot. I'll park a little farther away just so I can pull through. Do not hide in your spot. If your bike is buried deep in the spot, people might actually start turning in before they see it, and if they're in a hurry your bike could get tapped. Once you're in the stall, protect it by putting your bike in a visible position. Cars have to pull in to the end of the space because they're, what, potentially ten feet longer? You can't possibly need the entire length of a parking stall, but don't be afraid to take the extra space so it won't tempt someone. Don't hide your ride.

Think about inclines and grades. Parking lots have to drain so they are graded to run water off and out of the lot. That grading can be very, very shallow or it can be quite pronounced. Important tip: Never park with your nose downhill. If you're nose down against a curb or the bumper of a car, you're gonna have to back that bike uphill to get out. I always park level or nose up to avoid having to try and push backward up a hill.

What about parking downtown? Well, since everyone's going there, here are some things you might want to do. Start by checking with your city to see if there are any designated "Motorcycle Only" parking spots around. I know from experience that most universities and colleges have bike only parking spread around campus, and in my area, the city of Boise, Idaho, has motorcycle only spots on the streets downtown. In the information age you can often Google your city and look for parking maps and find those specialty parking places. If you're using a parking structure in a city you do have the choice of paying and using a full stall, but you might try talking to the attendant to see if there's a nook or a cranny you can park in for free. There's no guarantees, but I've shoved it in a corner for free before. You're taking up no space and actually freeing one up so it can't hurt to ask.

Flow of traffic in lots is very important. A parking lot is a cluttered and busy place where people are looking for open spots, not motorcycles. Have your head up and on a swivel. Watch the brake lights and reverse lights of cars in stalls. Remember if a parked car's brake lights come on, that means it's running and in order to pull the gear selector out of neutral the brakes have to be applied. That means the sequence of events inside that car are: sit down, key in, foot on brake, put in reverse, and pull out. You'll notice I didn't put a step called "look for oncoming traffic—especially motorcycles" in that mix. Why? Because people sitting in a car with their foot on the brake are putting it in reverse and then looking to see if they can see a car coming through the side windows of that van they parked next to. Remember how hard it is for you, in a car, in a parking space, to see oncoming traffic and act like you know you're hard to see. You might even consider running your brights during the day in a parking lot because you're just that much harder to see and increasing your visibility in a dangerous environment is a good idea.

As far as parallel parking, I'm willing to say park with your rear wheel to the curb, with your nose pointed with the flow of traffic. If you have concerns or worries that your local vehicle code may not allow that, call somebody who knows. I can't possibly know what your unique, individual, and independent civic authorities may have on the books.

Parking, like all the good parts of riding, requires a lot of personal responsibility. We need to be able to make our own decisions and live with the consequences. In Christianity there's concern about "the unforgivable sin," the idea that there is something that you can do that cannot be forgiven. Once, to put people's minds at rest, I heard a pastor on the radio say, "If you're worried you've committed the unpardonable sin, then clearly you haven't, because if you had you wouldn't care." I offer this completely opposite advice for your parking decisions—if you're worried you're going to get ticketed or towed, then don't park there, because odds are you should be ticketed or towed. In parking, if you think you're committing the unpardonable sin, you probably are. If you can stand up and take that ticket then park. If you can't, get back out in the lot with everybody else.

Cowboy up.

LANE POSITION

Ask me, "Crash, where should I be in the lane?" and I'll answer, "Yes. You should be in the lane. All of you."

You'll say, "What? The center?" and I'll answer, "Yes. It depends."

Then you'll ask, "What about the left third?" and I'll answer, "Yes. It depends."

About now you'll get angry and say, "What about the right third?" and I'll answer, "Yes. It depends."

As you start pouring nickels into a sock to beat me with you'll say, "So, anywhere in the lane is OK?" and I'll say, "Nope, it depends." At which point you swing your nickel-filled sock at me, I duck, and you whack yourself in the knee and go down like a cheap prost...I mean, house of cards.

One of the indefinable things that people always want from motorcycle professionals is a fixed rule, a statement of, "Always do this and you'll be OK." In the riding world there are very few absolutes, it is a mix and match kind of patchwork where you have to have some ability to adapt to your situation. The annoying thing is that people will pester you for an absolute answer, and then when you finally just give up and give them a hard and fast rule they start all this, "Yes, but what if?" crap that just drives you up a tree. The only people who live in a world with absolute right answers are politicians, and even they know they are lying about it.

Where should you be in a lane? I want to be where I can see the most, am most easily seen by others, and can keep as much space as possible to maneuver. Some call this "space cushion" or "having an out" or "mind the gap" but for me, my rule of thumb is I just want don't want to put myself in a box. A rule of thumb is a rule that comes from experience not from formal education. For example, a dietary rule of thumb wouldn't be about calories or grams it would be something like: Never eat anything bigger than your head. (Look, it's a good rule of thumb, yes?) A rule of thumb is easily and widely applied. It accepts its own ability to be varied—it means that generally you should or shouldn't do something, but that occasionally that rule can be broken. I ate some barbeque in Kansas City. The amount of food was probably larger than my head and I did, indeed, enjoy it...and the twelve hour nap I took afterwards. As a rule of thumb, however, I'm not gonna do that again...unless it's pork...and it's at Gates...then...well...new rule of thumb.

Rule of thumb for lane position: Don't put yourself in a box. This means physically having room to maneuver and visually being able to see as much as possible and be seen by as many as possible—don't hide in traffic—you want people to see you. Remember, as vehicles move in reference to your position their visual shadow shifts. That box truck that was next to you blocking your immediate left moves forward and then blocks your vision of vehicles in the center turn lane. If you can't see the center turn lane then someone waiting for the truck to pass so they can turn left can't see you. In a very real sense this is complex geometry that you need to be aware of and use to your advantage.

I used to be a TV news photographer and one time when I was a newbie shooter I arrived at a "man with a gun" standoff. The guy was irrational about a divorce or girlfriend or something. The police had the entire block cordoned off and were on and off the phone with the guy trying to talk him out. For his part, our barricaded gentleman was offering to shoot any officer that came to the door or maybe just shoot himself. When I arrived I found a really great vantage point not far from the house, about 50 yards away, with a clear view of the front windows. What a great shot, I thought, congratulating myself on being so close. I looked through the viewfinder and focused up a great shot of the front window and on cue these fingertips appeared at the end of the curtain and drew it back about six inches. I realized that I was getting a shot that was pure gold. Then, in a moment of pure clarity, I realized I was standing next to a tree in the open with a massive TV camera and tripod. Light bulb moment: I had a great shot, and he did too. I was exposed and had no cover. I moved the camera next to the tree and myself behind the tree.

Now, a word about assumptions, I assumed our broken-hearted barricade boy saw me. How could you not see big twenty-six pound TV camera on a tripod in the neighbor's front yard? It is possible that he was blinded by grief, or that he wasn't looking for TV cameras so he mentally missed me. He could have just glanced out and missed seeing me—I'll never know. An important point here is that even if you're in a lane position that gives and gets great visibility it doesn't mean that the people who can see you actually *do* see you. Sometimes they're looking for something else. Imagine the soccer mom on her way to pick up Skippy from karate class (Poor kid just gets beaten up all the time at school.) and she's trying to time it out so she can swing by and drop Veronica at that tap dance class before heading over to the bake sale at the football game; in what world is she thinking about and looking for motorcycles?

We are motorcyclists and *we* look for bikes, even in our cars we look to see brand and style and color and "What kind of exhaust is that?" We look for bikes to see if we need to wave or not wave—or, "Do I know that guy?" Think about how much time you spend looking for and at other motorcycles and then tell me what color was the last pickup truck you saw? See what I mean? We aren't invisible. We're off other users' radar. Because we're off the radar, we need to be aware that other users might want to be in the space we inhabit and be ready for it.

One thing that I have in my constant scan is other users' head positions. Are they staring straight ahead? If the gal in the Camry is up on my front right quarter and she suddenly looks left and then forward and then left again, she may be signaling her interest in my lane (or maybe she just has a twitch of some kind). It's my job to realize that she's oddly interested in my lane so I can decide if I need to back off, pull ahead, or just shift to the left of the lane and buy myself some space and time.

Clearly, there is no single best lane position to be in because of the fluid nature of traffic. Use a rule of thumb and stay where you can see, you can be seen, and you have maneuvering space if you need it. Oh, and play a little "but what if..." in your head to keep you on your toes and know your options. Just don't write me a letter and expect me to have the answer because you won't like it, "'cause it all depends."

Afterthought—If you want to talk about lane position in curves it is called "apexing and choosing a line." Go look it up in the table of contents. For this discussion we are talking about working in traffic and on fundamentally straight roads.

Hip to Swerve

A swerve is simply back-to-back countersteers with the intent of quickly changing your path to avoid an unforeseen obstacle. Basically it's a quick course correction and reset; you find something you need to immediately avoid so you swerve around it and return to your original path. I also believe it is a warning sign that you're following too close or are asleep at the wheel. Symptomatically a swerve is a startle reaction to an unforeseen pathway obstruction. (Holy Moly! That sounded positively clinical. I must be channeling the inner plastic surgeon or an ambulance chasing lawyer at least!)

I have a problem with folks who are constantly saying, "You have to be ready to swerve at any second." Then again, I've always had a hard time keeping my mouth shut when young ladies say things like, "There are no good guys around—all I can find is bums." Why? Because over half the time when they're saying these things they're in a bar or at a party where nobody is looking for long-term, serious relationships. If you're looking to buy oranges why in the world are you at a hardware store? Start by looking in a place where they actually sell what you want to buy. A swerve is a startle response. By its very definition, it is designed to avoid something that is suddenly in your way—call it a panic response or a startle response—the deal is the same: You were riding along fat, dumb, and happy and BOOM there's something in your direct path of travel that you have to avoid. If you had spotted it early it wouldn't require a swerve, it would require a "change of course" or an "adjustment of your path of travel," but not a swerve.

A good swerve is going to go like this: You press on the hand grip on the side of the direction you wish to swerve, you hold that press long enough to change your path of travel, and then you press on the other grip to return to your original path. A good swerve is a good quick S-turn that gets you around something by which you were caught off guard. Did I mention that if you're swerving it's because you've been caught out?

Cars, trucks, and SUVs have a really cool ability to simply drive over (straddle) things they don't want their tires to hit. Remember how you drive your car? You've straddled stuff before, you know you have! Most of the stuff we straddle while in our cars are smaller, less dangerous things. In my own vehicle I've straddled all sorts of lumber from plywood and door trim to 1x4s and 2x4s, even short chunks of 2x6s or larger—but once you get to 4x4s, even in our cars we start swerving. Think to that straddling moment a second, and you'll remember that moment of dread fear you had when, magically, something appeared out from under the car in front of you, followed by quick relief as you realized that, "If they drove over it—so can I."

Hold onto that moment of fear a second, that surprise and fear as suddenly, with just enough time to recognize what it was, you simply straddled it because that's what the guy in front of you did. Insert this into the equation now: you are on a motorcycle. Straddling is out the window and your choices are now surmount or swerve. An important and overlooked part of the swerve equation is following distance. An appropriate following distance will allow you the time to adjust your course without a violent swerve. I'm not saying you're not going to make a course adjustment; what I am saying is that if you are following too closely, and when the car you're following too closely straddles something, you are making a violent swerve necessary.

Think about this: You're following at what appears to be a normal distance for a car, about one second. Military fighter pilots have a startle response somewhere in the .4 second range, meaning when something happens in front of them, they can take action in about a half a second. We lesser mortals run closer to one to one and a half seconds to sight, process, and then start an action. If you're following another vehicle at one second, then you roughly have time to spot something appearing from under that car in front of you, realize it's in your path, recognize it is a shovel, and then, in your car, you straddle it because you're out of time.

What happens when you're on your bike? You see it. You recognize what it is. With luck you...surmount. If you're going to swerve you need the time and space to make that swerve work. Keeping a safe following distance gives you the space and time to react safely to things that pop out from under the vehicles in front of you. Speaking of space, when you swerve you need room to move, so make sure that you're aware of the traffic around you. If you are simply riding along, target locked on the license plate in front of you, and you're in the center lane position you probably have space to make a robust swerve to the right or left. If you're in the left lane position— think about this—then you have loads of room to swerve to the right. The only problem being that odds are, since that's the center of the lane, that's where the object you need to avoid is. Fortunately, although you're limited on space to the left, you probably don't need much because you're already out of the path of things that cars straddle.

Cars surmount things, too. They spit stuff out from under their tires, don't they? If you're in the right or left wheel track, you aren't guaranteed safety. An inattentive driver will run over things without hesitation. Try a flat cardboard box for example, or a sheet of plywood or fiberboard or drywall; all things a car will run over, no questions asked. Your bike will go over them, too, but it's not that much fun. Think about it. Is that new or used plywood? Used plywood can have nails and screws sticking out of it like thorns from a rose. You can surmount it very easily, but it can give you a nasty puncture in return. A little space, a little time, and a gentle swerve avoids all kinds of potential problems.

As well as the space and time to react, you need the skills. A swerve does need to be practiced. You should be practicing it in the parking lot, and if you're comfortable with it, on the road a little as well. The basics:

1.   Look where you want to go. Don't look at what you want to avoid. Look where your escape is.

2.   Know where other users are and how much room you have to maneuver in.

3.   Go in the direction that offers the most room and best chance to fully avoid the object.

4.   Press on the bar on the side of the direction you want to go. Hold the press long enough to avoid the object.

5.   Once you're clear press the other grip to return to path.

6.   Roll your hips. Yep, this is a quick move. Let the bike move under you, don't bother trying to lean with it. Roll them hips like you're doing the Hustle, Macarena, or whatever. This can actually be hard to do, because you're potentially nervous or freaked out. Practice will help.

7.   After you swerve and safely return to your path it's always important to ask yourself, "Self, why did that just happen?" Are you following too closely? Is there a dump truck up there ahead shedding schmutz all over the road?

The swerve is also a massive traction consumer. A quick braking maneuver can buy you a little space and time, but once you're swerving I would suggest that is all you should be doing. Balancing the demands of a swerve and braking at the same time is a delicate balancing act and in traffic it can end very, very badly. For me, this is a key part of the equation—potential outcomes; how do you end up in a mess? Ladies—how do you find the wrong guys? By being in the wrong place. I can swerve like a demon, and I practice every single time I ride (swerve around manhole covers), but I can't remember the last time I swerved because I had to. Then again, some people feel I don't follow as closely as I could...

SURFACE CONDITIONS

Sounds like a bad movie, doesn't it? "After a nuclear power plant suffers a terrible accident caused by a wealthy and reckless arms manufacturer; six scientists and a really, really hot marine biologist/morally safe character are trapped by bioengineered shark hybrids in an underwater research facility. Time and oxygen are running out as they debate how to best escape without becoming shark bait! Yet—even if they get out—what are the *surface conditions*!?!" Oh, it's just a red bikini top and khaki Daisy Dukes away from a hit. Wait, I'm not supposed to be mapping the comeback of a minor '80s television action hero. I am supposed to be talking about surface conditions. "Because even if they escape the blood thirsty hybrids, what nightmare mutant cannibal future awaits these brave souls? What are the *surface conditions*?" Sorry. All done. Past it now. Just gonna let it go...away...away...

When we ride there are a lot of cues we often ignore. A cue is a sign that something might be changing. For example, around here, where I live, crosswalk signals have a countdown; they literally countdown from about twenty seconds to zero to give pedestrians the ability to know when to hustle and get out of the street. That same countdown is a cue to me on my motorcycle that the light is about to change! I like to pay attention to the countdown when I'm approaching an intersection, especially if the traffic is flowing slowly. From my lane I can see the timer counting down for people crossing in the direction I'm going. If that baby is going 3, 2, 1, as I'm getting close, I know I need to speed up to catch the li...I mean, I can prepare to slow and make a stop because the light is about to change. Yeah, that's what I meant. The pedestrian crossing signals are a cue. They tell me where we're at in the cycle. (Those old-school green "Walk" and red "Stop" signals usually flash as they end their cycles...usually.) Again, this is a cue, not a command, and lights are subject to malfunction so use it to plan not to proceed.

Surface conditions give cues as to what is going on as well. If you've been to a motorcycle safety course you know that those two cues are color and texture. Wet pavement is darker than dry, shiny things are interesting but often slippery, and it's easy to spot where concrete meets asphalt. Those visual cues need to be things that you're actively searching for and be willing to act on. Even on a road you ride every day you should be able to look ahead and say, "That looks weird..." and start processing what you're approaching. Why does the surface look different? Has there been roadwork? Maybe there is a spill on the road or it could be as simple as the sprinklers at the muskrat meat packers are poorly adjusted and they're trying to grow the road instead of bluegrass. Your job as a rider is to be constantly gathering and processing information.

Generational question: Who said, "Fat, drunk, and stupid is no way to go through life, Son"? That's right. Dean Wormer. Unfortunately, he was two-thirds right about motorcycling. Drunk and/or stupid is no way to ride your bike. Yes, I tried to ride drunk once but was foiled by the gas cut-off switch, and I have ridden stupid a lot and been lucky enough to avoid disaster...but I have been tumbling down the street more than once thinking "that was stupid." Riding can be a wonderful, ethereal, enveloping moment where there's a purity of purpose that is hard to recreate; however, riding doesn't mean pointing a motorized vehicle down the road in blissful ignorance of the world around you. Sight see! You should be seeing the beauty of God's creation around you. Marvel at the wonder of it all. Suck it in! The optic nerve from your eye to your brain is about as big around as a two-year-old's little finger—*use it*. Use it to enjoy the world around you—remembering all the while that superhighway of information going to your brain isn't there to dull your nerves and send you to a peaceful nirvana. It's a pipeline of vital information delivered to your brain to keep you alive.

Let me put this simply: If something doesn't look right, ask why. If you can't figure out why the road looks like that up there, slow down a little 'til you know. It's like eating a tuna sandwich— if it doesn't look right, why risk it? You're better off knowing what's ahead than guessing what's ahead. Remember, live a little further in the future so you can control it when you get there; color and texture are cues that can help you do that...because before you escape your watery grave, be sure to check the *surface conditions*! (Starring that guy you recognize but don't know his name).

Body Positioning

One of the things I see a lot of questions about is "body positioning." Generally, newer riders start leaning and picking up some speed and then start thinking, "Boy, I'm really getting something done here. I'm bound to run out of lean pretty soon—better learn to hang off...I mean work on my body positioning." By no means is what I'm about to say intended as an insult. I am not calling your mother fat, nor am I doubting the size of the tiger in your trousers, but often when riders start asking about body positioning and hanging off they are really just saying, "I'm scared to lean any further."

There I said it. Wait, I take it back—make it: "When new riders start asking about body positioning and hanging off they are really just saying, 'I'm leaning as far as I dare.'"

That better? Your ego OK? We didn't skid your id? Everybody feel good about themselves? This is one of those soccer games where we ain't keeping score. The bottom line is when we talk about body positioning we're really talking about lean and (generally) how to go faster. From time to time we all speak in code, whether we mean to or not. In my experience those that want help with body position are generally having issues with comfort while cornering. You experienced guys, think about it a moment; who asks about hanging off? New guys, that's who, because as their speeds come up, their lean increases, and as lean increases so does uncertainty and fear.

Imagine echo-y sound effects as you read this: "Wow, I'm really hustling. Never been this fast on this road before.... Really leaning...Wonder when hard parts are going to scrape..."

The "advisory speed" sign says 30 mph and the speedo says 35 mph. Look out, Barry Sheene.

One of my earliest memories of watching someone actively try to hang off when they would have been better served learning to ride was back in 1981. I had a '78 Honda XL500S. (Piped, jetted, White Brothers clutch and swing arm—"more money than brains" was me!) I rode it like a chucklehead. I was on the thumb of San Francisco Bay, coming up Pescadero Road from the coast, and I caught a guy on an Yamaha RD400. Now, an RD was a very, very cool machine and I figured that this dude would wick it up and put a hurting on my one-lunged, dual-purpose bike. I kinda hung back because I figured if I tried to pass he'd just put a whipping on me, and I was young enough to think, "Boy, won't it be cool if I can hang with this guy a while...just shadow him!"

Shadow him I did. He was doing this thing with his body where he'd try and shift to the inside of the turn. He'd get the interior cheek off the seat, and the inside foot was pointed all skee-whumpus. Then at the end of the turn he'd kinda lurch up and move to the other side and try the same thing and—to be perfectly 1981 and politically incorrect— to my eighteen-year-old mind he was a total spaz. *Ungainly* is the word I'd use now. At that time, I was riding a stand up dirtbike. I didn't hang off or even try; I just rode the ding-dang bike straight up and down, leaning with the bike. That's all. I didn't really realize what he was trying to do until I was recounting the story later to a more experienced rider. Remember, this is 1981 and DEVO is cool, the New Wave has started, Punk is awake and alive, and Disco is dying. Meanwhile, there's this guy riding an RD in front of me like he's riding with an uncomfortable cucumber in his pants. What was I supposed to think? Eventually, I grew bored (and slightly frightened), so I turned the dial to nine and slapped a pass on this guy. Four turns later I lost sight of him and never saw him again. (I assume he safely navigated his way to Skyline Boulevard.)

I have seen that cluttered, confused, odd dance numerous times throughout thirty years of riding. Mildly amusing, it is like watching teens play dress up at the prom. The attempt to go all Randy Road Racer at 25 mph in a 25 mph corner is...well...endearing and looks almost as awkward as a gangly eighteen-year-old in an Armani tux with plastic shoes. Quaint...charming...naw...endearing. It's endearing, because in some way or form we've all been there trying to act a little more grown up than we really are.

Part of the joy of riding is discovering your limits. When you're riding you're constantly growing and expanding your abilities, as that happens you bump into some barriers, some physical, some mental. The hard part is distinguishing which is which, and what makes things worse is that your boundaries are actually expanding as you mature as a rider. The sudden urge to learn to hang off could be the real need to get your ass to a track and start riding like a demon in the appropriate environment, or it could mean that you're at a place where you're starting to expand your boundaries, but guess what? It's graduation from eighth grade, not college. By this I mean that if you're dragging hard parts and your front tire is scrubbed to the edge, the rear is shedding material that looks like rubber cement, and you're routinely smoking the rear coming out of turns, you're at a point where you should get off the street and think about riding where there are EMTs standing by and some seasoned pros to teach you.

If you've been riding for a few months and suddenly you're so fast you need to get that knee down? Ahhhh...prodigy, delusion, or hopeful over-estimation, I'm not sure but I'm pretty darn comfortable saying this: "Take the cake mix out of the box and bake the cake before you frost it."

If you're a new rider worried about getting one cheek off the seat and kissing the mirror and...good on you for being concerned about improving your riding. The problem is you're worried about frosting the cake before you've even beat the eggs. Feeling like you're fast isn't wrong—you are faster than you've ever been. You've been riding a motorcycle for a year for goodness sake; you are *beaucoup* faster than you were when you started! Any faster clearly is gonna require some serious hangin' off!—Not.

Hanging off and body position is gonna be frosting, not foundation. Seriously, think about it a moment—who hangs off, when do they do it, and why do they do it? Answers: 1. Racers. 2. Racing. 3. To maximize corner speed.

Are you really going that fast? I am an old canyon squid. That's what I did—went up to the hill to look for someone to mix it up with. Thinking about it now, putting a pass on a fast bike with a slow rider might have been the kind of thing that got me started looking for a race. I was, I will readily admit, a danger to myself and those around me. I passed over the double yellow and scared myself and the innocent passersby on more than one occasion. If I could get in the way back machine and talk to 1983 me, I'd slap me pretty good. Being a squid, I have a different take on things than most "safety professionals" I know—I've been the idiot, enjoyed being the idiot, and occasionally am still an idiot. (I prefer the term *Hooligan* now.)

After a year of terrorizing people in the tight stuff on a modded dirtbike, I moved up to a Suzuki GS550E that was, of course, piped, jetted and equipped with R compound tires. I used to go up the hill and hunt for larger, "faster" bikes to pass. Allow me to give you some predator's insight. If I came up behind a motorcyclist and was thinking about passing them, I would watch for two things in my target, line selection and rider confidence. Line selection is simple. A rider who consistently apexes early and runs wide at the exit is an inexperienced rider and easy pickin'—simply hold the outside line, and as they slow at the exit (they're going wide, they'll roll off), you make for the late apex and power it by them on the way out. Easy-peasy, because everything they're doing is driving them outside, so taking the inside line keeps you out of their way. (Trying to pass on the outside of a rider who is consistently running wide is, well, suicidal and stupid.)

Confidence is a different kettle of licorice. A rider braking past the apex? Scared. A rider who is trying to lean off when they don't need to? Scared. A rider who spends more time trying to look over his shoulder to see who's behind him and where they are? Scared. Poor throttle control, grabby braking, or trying to muscle the bike instead just riding it? Scared. Reading another rider's body language isn't as hard as you might think. We readily telegraph our level of comfort. Spotting a rider who can't sort out what they're doing is pretty easy. All it takes is a few turns and you'll see where the opening is going to be and be able to motor past.

Rather than get all "body-curious," if you're thinking it's time to hang off, go back and focus on the basics—line selection, good braking, throttle control, and appropriate entry speeds. Oh, and know how to steer your motorcycle; knowing to press on the inside grip to tighten your line is a lifesaver. All those things, those basic skills, are the eggs, flour, and sugar of your cake—make sure the basic ingredients are there, mixed, baked, and ready before you put on the icing.

Trust me, nothing is more fun that running up on a dude on a fast bike and frosting them with a hopped-up dirtbike. You want to avoid that being done to you? Then focus on the basics.

RAIN

People frequently ask about riding in the rain. From those conversations it appears to me that riders have a fundamental inability to distinguish rain from ice. Loads of riders seem to believe that if it rains all traction magically disappears and we wind up skittering cross the road like a bunny on a frozen lake, which is simply not the case. Granted, a light rain will lift grime and oil up and create a hazard for a short time, but after solid bit of raining and cleansing, there is a shocking amount of traction available in the rain.

When it rains it's not like the road gods cover the road with a shower curtain and pour out baby oil; it is still the same decent traction surface with a touch of water on top of it. Remember, liquid water and solid water have differing traction landscapes. *Rain* makes you slow down a tad and be wise; *ice* means we really should be videotaping this for a viral video. Unfortunately, due to rider legend, rain is like the Y2K of riding; overblown, over estimated, and driven by mythology. If you've ridden in a downpour you know that once you're out there in it, it doesn't have to be a big deal. Yeah, remember how you couldn't find a generator in a big box store in 1999? How everybody was buying up MREs and water distillers/purifiers? That's the kind of fear you conjure in many riders' minds when you say, "Looks like we'll be riding in the rain." Riders, especially less experienced ones, go all apocalyptic and freak out. Trust me, I've been there. In the world of motorcycle training there are really only two routine acts of nature which will cancel a class: lightning and ice. Why? Because they create an unsafe condition, and people can get hurt in a hurry—rain don't stop the show. Rain is just something that happens that you have to deal with.

Imagine being on a range with twelve new, wannabe riders and saying, "Yes, It's raining, and yes, we will be riding." Jaws drop, eyes get bigger, and eyebrows raise. You'd think you just said, "We will now take off all our clothes and compare body shapes." People get all weirded out.

"But...it's raining!" they say.

You reply, "Yes but you'll probably get caught out in the rain someday, and considering what we're doing is training, you'll be just fine."

"But it's raining!" they say again, this time they say *raining* really slow so you can understand that "it's raaaiiiinnnniiinnnngggg." In this situation here's what I do. I ask everybody to get up on the balls of their feet, to lift their heels into the air, and then I say, "Do the twist." Twelve puzzled people look at me, and I say, "Like this," and then attempt to do the twist with my feet, to rotate the balls of my feet, to make them slide around—you know like you did when you're a kid and you step out onto ice for the first time. Sometimes it takes a moment, but eventually everyone tries it, and surprise, there's a shocking amount of traction on wet asphalt. Walking out to the bikes, no one throws out a hip or goes skittering across the range as they stop next to their bike.

Rain is not the end of the world. In fact, during the rain, traction is kind of a secondary issue for me; the primary issue is vision and visibility. When it's raining it's harder to "see and be seen." Granted, my head is on a swivel, and I'm not going to ride across those big steel plates they cover excavations with unless I absolutely have to, but, friends, think about what you see from inside your car during a good soaker with the wipers going on high. It's not much, *and* what happens to your scan as you lean toward the windshield and peer into the storm? Once a body is in a car and the wipers are going, they are just about fixated on looking out the front and trying to see between swipes. If you need to replace those wipers it's even worse. From a visual perspective, the rain falls and impairs vision, the water from the road is splashed and sprayed by other users, also impairing vision, and your helmet does not have a windshield wiper so remember—you're working from a visual hole.

To me, a driver's impaired ability to see you in the rain is every bit as important, if not more so, than the minor traction issues you can easily manage. Managing traction in the rain is a case of looking for those clues that warn you of diminished traction. Plates, grates, and paint become potent low traction zones so avoid them. Puddled water can be hiding surface imperfections or potholes so don't go banging through standing water. Slow down and ford that lake.

True story: I was on my XL500 back in the day and decided to banzai it through this big puddle that I had been eyeing for a while. You know the kind, on the inside of the elbow of a turn; you just have to straighten the turn out and SPLOOSH! You're some kind of kamikaze penguin skipping through, like a rock Moses would have tossed to part the Red Sea. Yes, I did make a big splash—only because when the front end dropped into about eight inches of water it felt like someone had grabbed the front brake. Over the nose I went, like some kind of kamikaze penguin skipping through the water sans motorcycle. The only thing that would have made it better and more ironic and embarrassing was if a bus load of cheerleaders had been there to see it. Fortunately, my shame was mine and mine alone. I don't know how, but I picked the bike up out of the water, let it drain a moment, and that dang thing re-fired no questions asked. Shivering my way home, I learned an important puddle killing lesson: Water in any kind of depth is like pudding, get the front wheel *up* before you hit the water. Simply put, deep standing water can be a hazard in itself.

Things to remember:

1.   Rain will make the road surface snotty in the first few minutes of a rainstorm. After a few minutes it will rinse the road clean. Feel free to slow down or even stop and let the road get a quick baptism and cleaning.

2.   Rain will make low traction surfaces even more dangerous. Beware of painted arrows, manhole covers, steel plates, polished concrete, or any other surface that is usually slick—rain will make it worse.

3.   Vision, both yours and others, can be greatly diminished. It's harder to see in the rain and it can rain hard enough that people will actually *stop* driving. Be aware if you're having trouble seeing then others are having trouble seeing you. If the visibility is such that it's dangerous to continue, find a safe place to pull off and seek shelter. You do not want to be powering along in a hard rain only to find that traffic is stopped in front of you.

4.   Live in the future. If you see a massive thunderhead in your path you do not have to punch a hole in it. You can go around some storms, and for others you can park up and see which way they are headed and out-wait them. If entering a storm is unavoidable, keep your wits and be ready to look for and accept shelter.

5.   Be ready for the conditions. Even in the summer, if you are wet and cold you can end up hypothermic, meaning your body starts getting too cold, your core temperature goes down, and things like the shakes take over. Your judgment and short term memory become impaired, you are a danger to yourself and others—start smart and carry your rain gear. Put it on before you need it, not after.

Rain doesn't have to be a rider's enemy. It is a natural

occurrence and not the end of the world. Rain increases the need to be alert, aware, and careful but doesn't mean an automatic crash. The key to surviving rain is respecting it, not fearing it. Vision is compromised and traction as well. You need to slow down, increase your following distance, and give yourself more time and more space.

When I started writing this piece, I was watching the sixth stage of the 2011 Tour de France and it was pouring rain...and they kept riding. When I was watching the Assen MotoGP race broadcast from Holland this year, it was pouring rain but they raced anyway. Rain isn't the problem. The problem is when we don't change our behaviors to deal with it.

GROOVY PAVEMENT

There are a couple advantages that riders who start in the dirt carry over riders who start on the road. One is that dirt riders are much more comfortable with the handlebars being "alive" in their hands. By *alive* I mean the bars are twitching and flexing in your hands. On a trail the front wheel hunts, it bounces around, is deflected by rocks and roots—it turns in your hands. By staying loose and alert on the bars dirt riders learn that gentle control and continued power to the rear wheel will allow the bike to keep going in a straight line, even if the bars are flopping around in their hands. That simple hint, that the bars are alive and when going in a straight line (and even in some turning situations) it's OK for them to be giving you loads of feedback, puts dirt riders into a situation that if the bars twitch they do not make things worse.

When you're riding down the highway you may encounter groovy pavement. I'm talking about grooves cut parallel to your path of travel that are there to create better traction in the rain. Unfortunately, they have a knack for grabbing your tires and giving them a little wigglin'. A dirt-trained rider will simply react the way he always has on the trail: with a firm relaxed grip. A street-trained rider can get pretty freaked, get a death grip on the bars, lock his elbows, and start fighting it. Which answer sounds appropriate to you? Yup, firm and relaxed. You can get away with the death grip, locked elbow thing, but, man, will it tucker you out.

When we speak of things like grooved pavement we run the risk of getting sucked down the rabbit hole and having a "Yes, but what if..." conversation. You know, "Yes, but what if the grooves in the pavement are from grinding down uneven road surface—what then?" Ahhh, how about a firm, relaxed grip? "Yes," you say, "but what if it's intermittent? You know. They ground off all the high spots, and there's a patch of ground off stuff and then clean asphalt and then ground off stuff—what then?"

How 'bout a firm, relaxed grip?

"But, what if there's a turn, and they've ground off the pavement all through the turn—then what?"

How 'bout a firm, relaxed grip? Countersteer as necessary. Look through the turn. Since you're an alert and aware rider you probably saw the change in surface coming so you slowed a little...

"OK," you say, "but what if it's not ground off to even the surface? What it it's ground off so they can lay another layer of asphalt on top of an existing one?"

Ahhh...firm and relaxed? See, I can do this all day long. Whatever permutation of grooved pavement you can imagine, I'm gonna give you the "firm but relaxed" answer. See, a firm grip on the bars with relaxed arms is gonna get you through a lot of hassles. Why? Because the front axle is alive; it's active. It will make minor deflections and then come right back into line; I'm not talking about taking your hands off the bars and hoping for the best, and I'm not talking about squeezing the grips so hard you leave marks. I mean a firm grip and relaxed arms. Don't try to choke the bike to death and don't lock your elbows.

How you react to things like rough pavement will define

how the bike reacts. If you're cool, the bike's cool. If you get to fighting things and freaking out, so does the bike.

Ever heard this before? "An object at rest stays at rest, and an object in motion stays in motion with the same speed and in the same direction, unless acted upon by an unbalanced force." Well, your bike is in motion, and minor forces are nipping at the front wheel. Where could an unbalanced force come from? What? You've never thought of yourself as an unbalanced force before? Strange, ain't it. We tend to think of ourselves as a balancing force on a motorcycle, the thing that keeps it stable and upright. Not so much. Remember ghost riding that bicycle when you were in middle school? Them things will ghost ride for a long time if you can get them going fast enough.

OK, I'll admit to ghost riding pedal bikes into brick walls— but it was all in the name of science! "Look guys! Newton was right! Wow, that wall sure was an unbalanced force and certainly acted upon that Stingray." Juvenile? Yes. Evil? No. Kids know that if you get a two-wheeled vehicle going with any amount of speed (motion), it will stay in motion until gravity and friction do their thing...or the side of a school house blocks its path. Kids know stuff, and if you remember some of that stuff you knew as a kid it'll make you a better rider. Hey! Remember riding your bike no-handed? Don't do that on your motorcycle—not because it doesn't work (I didn't tell you that.), but because it's dangerous.

Ask an instructor about what it takes to ride and many will instinctively ask you, "Can you ride a bicycle?" Ostentatiously it's a balance question and given and taken as such. In reality there is a subtext that is really important: A motorcycle, at its core and its genesis, is really just a motorized bicycle. Sorry. It is. The difference is the power plant.

Think back to the days when you rode your bike over rough surfaces. Did you lock your arms straight and try to choke the grips to death, or did you just keep riding? For most situations where the roadway surface appears compromised, you need to slow and assess the situation and then, with a firm, relaxed grip, keep riding. If you're worried about traction, then slow and don't make sudden inputs. It's the same dang thing you did as a kid.

Wait. I can hear it. You've got a "Yes, but..." Guess what I'm gonna say? Firm, relaxed, no sudden inputs, be smooth—this is a rule of thumb and generally it's gonna be the right move. Don't make riding harder than it needs to be. Stuff that worked when you were ten years old still works today. Remember, no matter what happens keep riding the motorcycle.

Voids, Cracks, and Railroad Tracks

OK, it should be potholes, cracks, and railroad tracks but voids has a better ring to it, don't ya think? And what is a pothole but a void, an empty space, a missing something, a place where there once was but now isn't...kinda like how green onions disappeared from Nacho Belle Grandes. Either way, we're talking about things that upset and unsettle the front wheel of your motorcycle, which nicely sets up our first important tip: The front wheel will get knicked, whacked, and whanged, causing it to deflect momentarily. The wheel wants to return to track true, if you have a firm but relaxed grip on the bars 999 times out of 1000 the wheel simply comes back on track. In one in a thousand you'll get a nasty twist and may have to consciously steer the bike back on path.

There has to be a confluence of events to have a pothole, crack, or railroad track take you down. First, you have to be completely oblivious to your surroundings. Almost all the chains of events that lead to you sliding around on the ground start with you not knowing what's going on around you and being caught by surprise. Remember what your buddies always say after a crash, "I don't know what happened...must have been some oil or gravel I didn't see." BS. Interpret that as, "I was riding along totally clueless, and then something happened...so I made it worse with a nasty brake/throttle/steering input."

The easiest way to solve a problem is to not let it become a problem. Keep your head in the game and your eyes well ahead. Oddly, potholes will somehow magically appear from underneath cars. If you're following too closely you won't have time to react—you'll simply see the pothole before you hit it. Increase your following distance a touch. *Oh,* wait...you want to know what to do if you can't avoid it? It's an inverse surmounting, so you do the same thing as when you ride over a cat...sup bottle, a plastic catsup bottle...yeah that's it. Get up on the pegs if you can, firm relaxed grip on the bars, on the gas as you strike it, off the gas as you clear it, head and eyes up, looking well ahead.

But wouldn't it be easier to just make a gentle swerve around it? I'm always impressed by how many riders make riding harder than it needs to be—sure, you should know how to ride through a pothole. You are going to be asleep at the switch sometime and, yes, you will have to ride through or over something you didn't expect. Nobody is perfect. Nobody sees everything that's coming. Some riders get caught in a loop of "what if" and start adding complications to a situation in some strange attempt to create a no-win. I don't understand that. Obsessing about a scenario isn't a good idea—you're better served to have the basics down pat—because you can't possibly in a million years ever dream up every variation and have a plan of action for it.

Anything that wants to deflect the front wheel needs to be a concern, if you're not keeping an eye on the road surface you're in a hole to start with. Having both hands on the bars will help if something unexpected happens. Yeah, I ride one handed once in a while—I stretch out, relax, flex—but I wouldn't take a hand off the bars unless I was absolutely sure I could see the surface rolling up to meet me.

Cracks, seams, and edges often run perpendicular to our paths. We generally just ignore them, the front pops over them, the suspension does its job and absorbs them and we keep on rolling. A crack or seam that is parallel isn't a real problem, until you decide you need to cross over it. A crack or seam isn't a big issue, unless it's a *big* issue—a tall edge will deflect the tire and potentially you won't be able to surmount the edge and travel over it. *If* you have a seam or crack with a high edge, I would strongly suggest waiting to try and cross it until it is minimal, and then cross it as close to perpendicular as you can. That may mean a thirty or forty degree angle instead of a right angle, but you want the wheel to travel *over* the imperfection instead of grinding *along* it. Every once in a while I've had a seam that simply starts working its way across my lane. In other words, the seam doesn't run parallel with my path; it runs nearly parallel and slowly converges with one side of the lane or the other. If a seam is choking your lane out, make lemonade out of lemons; you've got a couple extra degrees to add to the equation to make things closer to perpendicular. Look for a place where the seam looks narrowest and lowest and then make your cut over.

Rules of thumb: First, potholes are inverse surmounting. You get on the throttle to lighten the front so it won't drop as hard into the void, you brace yourself, get a little more suspension action out of your legs if you can, keep looking where you want to go—but aren't you better off avoiding them? Second, seams, cracks, and edges are a problem and you should try to avoid them, if you can't then cross them as close to ninety degrees as you can get.

Railroad and trolley tracks are the same as a crack or seam, get your bad self across them as close to ninety degrees as possible. I know I'm not breaking any new ground here; there is no "OMG" moment, no shining epiphany, where the doors of enlightenment open and you say, "I never thought of that!"

If you want to really scrutinize what an expert rider does then watch their basics; the fundamentals are there and intact. Ever hear people talk about an expert rider? The key word they use is *smooth*. It's a beautiful compliment if you ever get it. Why do we notice the smooth? Because so many of us ain't. We're rough. We're awkward. We're reactive. Expert riders are smooth, because while we're living in the present, they are living in the future. In the world of expert riding, we're watching a plan was formulated fourteen seconds ago. We get to see it happen in what was their past—the event is already over when we see it.

Cracks, gaps, seams, trolley, and rail tracks—all those things shouldn't be surprises. Back off so you can see more. Keep your head up. Scan and plan. If you see a problem fourteen seconds ahead, you can avoid it, or at least have a kick-ass plan when you get there.

RIDING OVER STUFF
(SURMOUNTING)

Sometimes you find yourself riding your bike like you drive your car: brain dead, you know, just following the license plate in front of you. Your processor is off. You're just flying autopilot and thinking about what's gonna be good for dinner and things like that. Things like, "If you ask a man what 'swag' is he will tell you it's free stuff from a client or manufacturer; yet, when you ask a woman what 'swag' is she'll tell you it's a window treatment."

And suddenly there's a shovel laying full across your lane, effectively blocking your path. Hello, Mr. Shovel, what are you doing there? Where did you come from? Are you a landscaping shovel? A digger of ditches? A scooper of poop? Suburban gardener's tool or construction companion, there's six feet of oak/fiberglass/unknown lesser wood with a pointy metal spade laying in your lane, and about the time you see it is about the time you're gonna strike it.

In the perfect world of motorcycle safety training every event like this somehow magically happens twelve to fourteen seconds ahead, and you have a beautiful plan to evade, and if you can't you have enough time to pull up a quick laundry list of what to do and execute it. Yup, you can rummage around in the dusty corners (where the watercolor memories are) and fetch up that "how to" and review it before you have to: rise up off the seat, bend your knees, roll on the throttle, and then roll off after surmounting. Easy peazy lemon squeezy!

Or not. Because realistically if you have the time to shake off the cobwebs, find the info, and act, then you probably had time to change lanes and go around the shovel. Yeah, if you're running crap over, then you're running behind the curve and you're in reaction mode, not proactive mode. Having to surmount is a symptom of a failure in your awareness—but that's OK! Because, I am your friend. I understand that we all end up asleep at the switch and can find ourselves in a tight spot. It's OK, Spanky—you're human—the issue is are you ready to act and get yourself out of this bind you've found yourself in?

Surmounting is one of those things you may or may not ever have to do. I have surmounted things...furry things...a squirrel and a slightly larger mammal. Both times my options were to make some crazy steering and braking inputs or get on the gas and get over it. I chose the throttle. Why? Because if it's a case of me or an acorn thievin', furry-tailed rat, I'm going to choose me every time. (Yes, and what you fear I mean, I do indeed, mean.) If it's me or the cat, sorry Sylvester. That's the way I roll. I'm not trying to be cruel but in the world of riding you need to make quick, reasoned decisions, and for me, *I'm* the important quantity.

You are actually "surmounting" things all the time. You know that "abrupt edge"—that three inch step up from the old pavement to the new? You may have just "rode over" it but in Safety World you just "surmounted it." Ever accidently popped yourself over a small curb? Surmounted. Looked down and said, "Oops," as you rode over Junior's skateboard or hockey stick in the garage? Surmounted. Got a nasty lip going into the parking lot at work? Surmounted. Heck, even riding over the extension cord or garden hose is surmounting them. The deal is that you have ridden over things before, usually unintended and unexpected, so when you come upon a shovel on the freeway and you're in no position to avoid it, do what you've done before when you had no choice but to step up onto the new pavement: get your weight back, use your legs as shock absorbers, roll on as you strike it, roll off as you go over, head and eyes up, looking well ahead. In other words, just keep riding the bike.

Riding at Night

During the late summer, when it's been a million degrees all day, I like to go for rides in the evenings after the sun goes down. For me, there's something about riding around at ten or eleven at night in 70 and 80 degree temperatures that I just enjoy. Riding downtown, in the blue of the neon and the yellow sodium lights is fun. Cold nights are not much fun to ride in; your single goal is to get out of the cold which invades and nips at you. Sure a cold night can be invigorating, but there's always that sharp edge where frigid slips in and just reminds you that something hurtful is out there. Warm nights are different somehow, more enveloping; if it's right, it's a bit like being in a pool when the water's neither cold or hot, but just at that place where it's pleasant.

It's also very dangerous, because as well as being slightly anesthetized, you're out in the dark! And the places I like at night—main drag, well-lit areas—are surrounded by pin point lights. Other users can have a hard time picking you out of the mass of colors. Think about it. When you're out in the boonies and there's nothing but road, stars, and darkness your headlight is a beacon marking your arrival as it attracts moths, mosquitoes, and attention. When you're downtown, or even going by the strip mall, you're just part of the blur and action. Your headlight and tail light blend into the sea of signs and street lamps making you part of the landscape. Instead of popping out of it, you become just another glittering jewel in a tapestry of light.

Some folks deal with the danger of riding at night by simply saying, "Don't." That's probably a good idea; but I have to be honest, if you ride to or from work and you're a year-round or near-year-round rider you are probably going to be out in the darkness. Rather than encourage you to catch a cab or ride the bus, let me offer some simple ideas for riding at night.

1.   Increase your visibility as much as you can, perhaps with a retro-reflective vest. You see more and more of these out there nowadays, and having one in your saddlebag or under the seat could come in handy when you're watching the game and it goes into overtime. Bust it out; put it on. It certainly won't hurt.

2.   Be ready to adjust your route. Yup, try and decide where you're going to be most visible. Are you better off on a well-lit main drag with fifty thousand other lights, or going a little scenic and being the only oncoming light? (Got no research on that, so I can't tell you which is "safer." All I can tell you is as a rider you should consider it.)

3.   Remember that around dusk and dawn other users may or may not have their headlights on; act accordingly. Keep your head up and keep searching for dangers.

4.   Don't tailgate. Use other light sources to your advantage. Drop back a little, put the edge of your light on the bumper of the car in front of you, then look well ahead— meaning use the car in front of you as an extra set of lights. Instead of staring at the pool of light created by your light, look to the illuminated road in front of the user in front of you. (Little secret? On rural roads I like to have a car in front

of me lighting the way. I do not pass at night because why get ahead of your pathfinder?)

5. Never forget that the bright lights on a bike are pointed forward, so what does the back look like? How do you appear to someone approaching behind you? A quick tap or two on the brakes may warn that user that you're not part of a car. You're a motorcycle. To someone approaching from behind you may simply appear to be part of the tail lights of the car in front of you. Tap the brakes, move about in the lane a little, and try to avoid parking yourself centered behind a car at an intersection; that license plate of yours could be mistaken for the car's and, well, every car since the mid 80s has a third taillight back about where yours is sitting. To put it simply, don't hide in plain sight.

6. Hyper-vigilance—Things can come out of the darkness, things like kids on bikes, skateboards, cars with low or no lights, animals—all the dangers you'd find in the light, just a lot harder to notice. I was riding down El Camino Real in the city of Mountain View, California, one night and as I passed a bowling alley, a bowling ball crossed my path directly in front of me. At the time my nineteen-year-old mind said, "Coool...bowling for cars...neat idea!" Now? Well, trying *not* to hit cars seems like it would be more of a challenge. Keep your head and eyes up!

When we released the first book, I got the opportunity to go to Daytona and hang out a little during Bike Week. It was a gas. The only bike ride I got in on was a late evening/night ride on a CB350. Great little bike, neat ride. We wound up out in the countryside. I was following Mike, my publisher, and I'll be honest—it's dark as hell in Florida at night, and boy was I happy to let someone else who knew the place take the lead.

For me, part of the allure of riding at night is the increased challenge, but in my heart it's the other worldly aspects of riding on a dark summer's night that I find intriguing and dead sexy. Maybe that fusion of danger and fun is the thing that does it for me—it's like that mix of naughty and nice that makes for a good marriage. Thank goodness, I've got both.

CITY TRAFFIC

Ever watch hockey at home on TV? It's great. Loads of
action, "beverages" don't cost eight dollars, nobody spills
nachos on your crotch, *and* there's (usually) never a line at the
restroom. As nice as watching in your own home is, watching
in person is actually better. When I was a younger man a
couple of years out of high school, I lived with a gracious
Aunt and Uncle in Santa Monica, California. My cousin and
I would go to the LA Forum and buy cheap seats to watch the
LA Kings play. I even got to see Gretsky play when he was
with the Oilers. It was fun. As a California boy I had no idea
how hockey was played. It took some doing.

May I suggest, before your first game you learn a couple
of things: what and where the blue lines are, the definition of
"offside," and what "icing" is. Just like you need a rudimentary
grasp of the rules to enjoy a hockey game, before you go into
city or suburban traffic it's good to know a couple rules and a
couple tips to enjoy your ride more.

Traffic is a scary place, because as a rider you're the most
exposed person out there. To quote more knowledgeable
sources: On a motorcycle you are the crumple zone. You're

harder to see and often have a hard time seeing what's going on around you. In a lot of ways you're at a disadvantage because a mistake that would leave a dent in a car can leave you on crutches (or worse) for months. Frankly put, on a bike when it goes wrong it can go wrong *big*.

Which is why "situational awareness" is so dang important. Knowing what's going on around you, having a good, educated guess as to what is going to happen, and having a few options in your tool bag is so very vital. Blithefully going out into traffic, figuring your gonna do the usual thing you do in your car, is a recipe for wrecking. Remember, in traffic you're in a herd of four to eighty thousand pound vehicles that can't do much to avoid the guy who's rolling on the ground in front of them. High risk environment doesn't really cover it—riding in traffic is somehow more than just the regular dangerous. Part of that comes from the fact that you've been part of the pondering herd; you've been trained to drive a car in traffic. You have bad habits like staring at the license plate in front of you. If you bang another car then you pull over, exchange information, and pocket the fix-it money if you can.

On a bike, a fender bender is a broken leg, which is why it's important to remember hockey. Hockey rewards situational awareness—where the puck is, where you are, and where the other guys are. I know this makes me a sick and evil person, but during a hockey game one of my favorite things to see is when a player gets so absorbed in play that he forgets there are eleven other guys on the ice with him, and six of them really want to put a hurting on him. It is in that moment when a player has the puck and is looking to get that score, in that pure moment of focus, of thrill of the kill, that's when I love to see him get drilled by a defenseman who, seemingly, comes out of nowhere. See, when a player loses his situational awareness is when he becomes vulnerable. It's when the other team's enforcer realizes he's got a free shot coming. He loads the cannon and then BOOM! Highlight for the night.

I'm not saying that in traffic there are people who are out

to hurt you, but I am saying that in traffic if you get so fixated on something that you forget to note where the other players are or what they are doing, you're looking to have the hammer fall on you. If you get so locked on trying to get into that space in that lane that you stop paying attention to other users, then you're walking down the tracks with your eyes closed. You're standing in the path of the pain train as it leaves the station.

The enemy of situational awareness is target fixation. Legend is that during World War Two it was found that dive bomber pilots would get so fixated on putting their bombs on target that they would literally fly their planes into the target. Remember, a dive bomber gets above the target, gets into a steep dive, and then once on line and at speed he releases his bomb, pulls up, and flys home. Target-fixated dive bombers would concentrate so intently on the target that they forgot to pay attention to things like altitude—which when you're dive bombing things is really, really important because you need to pull up before you plow in.

That explained, a hockey player with a strong fixation on the net, or a pathway to it, can be extremely vulnerable to getting slobberknocked. (Slobberknocking is an old football term meaning you stick someone so hard that the slobber flies out of their face.) A good blindside hockey slobberknocker will spill a lot of beer as everyone jumps and goes, "WHOOOOAAAA!"

You can get slobberknocked in traffic. You can get so focused on one thing, you'll miss important clues about what's going on around you. Here's a couple of suggestions to avoid getting stuffed.

1. Head and eyes up and looking ahead *and* around— Look that twelve to fourteen seconds into the future. Know what's coming and who is where. Avoid surprises. Surprises are usually bad and indicate that you're not aware of your surroundings. Maneuver to keep a wide field of vision. You might consider following at a greater distance to improve vision and give yourself more reaction time.

2.   Keep your head on a swivel.—Yeah, your elementary, middle, and high school coaches were right. Look around and keep situationally aware. Have a scan pattern and use it—front, left, right, mirrors, near, and far. Know where other users are and where they appear to be going. This allows you to prioritize problems and threats.

3.   Watch for clues.—A car trying to exit a parking lot is a dangerous thing, especially if it's not signaling its intentions. The blinkers may not be on, but the driver will be giving clues like pre-turning the wheel in the direction he wants to go. Here's another: Say you're approaching a car looking to enter the road from your right. If all you see is the back of the other driver's head, if he is watching what is oncoming traffic to you, and he glances at you once in a while, he is looking to turn left across your path. Have a plan if he launches early *or* maybe if you're getting close, tap the horn. Let him know you are there.

4.   Communicate with other users.—You'd rather tap the horn than tap a fender. You might think you're being offensive, but the first time you honk and see a big surprised head turn and the wide, startled eyes of a driver realizing you are there makes it worth it.

5.   Know your right of way.—Protect your right of way. At a stop sign or stop light if you're in the right lane don't land in the far left side, because you're inviting right-turning traffic to pass you on the right. *Or* if you come up in the far right, other drivers may suppose you're turning right and try to pass you on the left to go straight.

6.   Realize your size.—You may have the right of way, but you're still the most exposed, vulnerable user out there, short of someone on a Segway who's out in traffic. If a chain-smoking, beehive-hairdoed, horn-rimmed, 1955 librarian wants to park her Edsel on top of your right of way, let her. Why? Because even though you get to shake your fist and yell, "I HAD THE RIGHT OF WAY!" from the strapped down safety and comfort of a backboard, you don't want to be the

guy who was right and injured. You want to be the guy who was offended but survived.

7. Blind spots—We all have blind spots on the bike, places we cannot see unless we turn our heads. Cars have blind spots, too, and you should stay out of them. A good way to tell if you're in a car's blind spot is age-old motorcycling advice: "If you can't see their eyes, then they cannot see you." Avoid placing yourself in other people's blind spots. Look at rear and side view mirrors to see if you can be seen. That goes for users on your right and your left. (Other riders also have blind spots *and* rearview mirrors so use those to position yourself around other riders as well.)

8. Visual shadows—Every vehicle throws a "visual shadow,"—a blocking space you cannot see through. This is a bit of optics and geometry and doesn't need to be as complex as it might sound. Consider this: You're following a RV. Because you're directly behind, it blocks the vision of your path of travel. Now, remember hockey? In hockey when there is a breakaway and a lone player is attacking the goal the goalie will come out of the goal to "cut down the angle." If you pause your playback here and imagine a cone extending from the player to the goal posts you'll see it's a triangle. As the goalie comes out of the goal, he fills the triangle more— cutting down the angle. Likewise, when you are following a large vehicle, dropping back gives you a greater field of vision. You drop back and decrease the amount of visual shadow that vehicle is throwing. Also, feel free to use your entire lane to move around and get a better look if your vision is blocked. Any moving vehicle is going to cast a moving blind spot (visual shadow) that you need to be aware of and be willing to account for and manage. Imagine a two lane road with a center turn lane. A car sitting in the center lane waiting to left turn is blocking your view of the oncoming traffic—a car traveling your same speed can be fully blocked and you will never see it if this times out right...or wrong, as it were. You need to remember some of that high school geometry and

astronomy and realize that moving bodies on the road can eclipse other riders.

9.   Have a plan.—Always have a plan. I'm not talking about where you're going and when you are going and what shirt you're wearing. I'm talking about while you are in city traffic you should be anticipating the actions of others and how you are going to react.

One more hockey story: One day I got a call on the phone and was invited to run camera for the local pro hockey team. (Boise has a team in the East Coast Hockey League.) I learned something important and that is this: When the puck is against the boards on your near side of the ice you cannot see the puck at all. Yup, it's true, completely visually blocked. Which is why, when you're the camera op, you learn a little trick; you watch the other players. They will flow to the puck. The player with the puck will look where he wants to go. On the chance that the puck gets jammed into a dogpile, there will be a couple of players hanging out just for that eventuality. Watch them. The same goes for traffic in the city, if you are blocked or have a visual shadow, take the time to notice what the other folks are doing—where are they looking; how are they handling their lane positioning? You need to be awake, alert, and aware of what's going on around you. Every bit of information can be helpful. Do not fall into the trap of just staring at the bumper in front of you.

TRUCKS

I like semis. I like big trucks. At one point I drove trucks. I started when I was sixteen on small dump trucks and then worked my way up, driving flatbed semis by the time I was eighteen. Successfully controlling anything of size and consequence is fun, and making 80,000 pounds of anything go where you want it to go and do what you want it to do is intensely satisfying. Once you've been out on the freeway and you're in very close proximity of another behemoth you learn to stay calm and trust the other guy. Close-quarter driving—when you're side by side for a moment, sharing the same air pocket, and you can reach out and touch the other truck—is an amazing feeling. When you worry you're gonna click mirrors as you push past or get passed, that is the kind of thing that makes you feel really alive. You're so in the moment and alert. It's hard to explain if you haven't been there. Close-quarter on bikes is the same sort of thing, but somehow the simple mass of the trucks changes things. It's hard to express.

For motorcyclists, trucks present a couple of problems. First, there's the problem of visibility. Trucks are large and hard to see around. They throw what I call a "large visual shadow," taking up a lot of the scenery and making it difficult to see things like road surface and other users. The first strategy is simple: avoid trucks. Stay out of their way. Trucks can have large blind spots and you are small, so the math is pretty easy—don't get too close. Keeping your distance also helps with vision. Take your hand and hold it right up in front of your face a couple of inches from your nose. You are now blocking your "field of vision," which is the actual full vision of things you can see. Your field of vision is taken up by your hand. Now, move your hand away from your face. Not down but away, you want to increase the distance between your hand and your nose. As a percentage, your hand is taking up less of your field of vision—you still can't see through it but you can see around it. Making sense? When you're around a truck or a RV, or even a van or SUV, you do not want to tailgate them because it cuts down on your field of vision. By keeping a decent following distance you can see more, and as always, have more time to react when that folded up lawn chair appears out from under that Kenworth.

Myself, I like to stay in the left third of the lane, situation permitting, because when far enough back I can actually see in front of a semi pretty well. I will then pass when the opportunity presents itself. There's nothing wrong with creating distance behind you to get a safety cushion between you and a large vehicle. Distance is time, and time gives you the chance to react appropriately if the other user makes a foolish move. The two dumbest places you can put yourself in proximity to a truck are directly behind it tailgating, and right next to the drive axles. The drive axles ("drivers") are the second and third axles of a three axle truck. Tailgating or being on the "drivers" puts you in a nasty blind spot where drivers have a heck of a time knowing you're there. It's a recipe for disaster. I've seen and had riders park it alongside a trailer, I'm assuming to take advantage of the shade or the wind block, and I'm here to say—driver's don't like that either—it's dumb; don't do it.

Trucks create another problem and that's turbulence. I was going to call it a "truck wake" but I believe turbulence covers it more appropriately. I made this decision at the Golden Gate National Recreation Area, which is a large area north of the Golden Gate Bridge that used to house artillery and observation posts for the defense of San Francisco back during the first and second world wars. The embattlements have outstanding views of the city, the bridge, the bay, and the open ocean. There is a point where you can stand and look back at the Golden Gate, see the city, and watch maritime traffic come in and out of the bay. The headlands are high enough you're looking down on the whole panorama. I was there with my brother because he really enjoys the area, and I now see why.

While I was there, I watched a couple container ships and an oil tanker or two come and go. The amazing thing to me wasn't that these trucks of the sea threw a wake, it was how quickly that wake was swallowed up by the natural wave action and turbulence of the sea. The bow wake was clear and the stern wake was readily visible, but after a few hundred feet the wake had been absorbed back into the natural motion of the ocean. Now, I know that not every ocean surface is as active as the pacific was that day—the wind was strong, there were whitecaps on the bay—but that's what made the wake issue stick out to me to this day. Every day is different, but some things never change. Trucks on the road throw a wake— get on a two lane state highway, pass one going 65 the other way, and you will feel it. If you're in close, you'll really feel it but, if you get farther away the turbulence of the atmosphere will start to absorb that turbulence, and the effect of the truck will lessen the further you get from it, which is why if you give plenty of room to a truck going the other way sometimes the wind blast is negligible.

I'm told that in the Gulf of Oman and other places that people surf on the wakes of supertankers. Sounds pretty dang cool. I've seen video of it on the web, and I've noticed that they stay pretty dang close to the supertankers because the farther away they are, the less of a wave there is. Surfers stay close for a simple reason—to get the most out of the wake thrown by the tanker before it dissipates back into the sea. The lesson for riders is simple: The turbulence caused by trucks is worse the closer to the truck you are, so give trucks a wide berth. I've had trucks go by me when the wind is right and it's like getting smacked; a good one will make you grunt. That one simple rule (give trucks a wide berth) will solve your vision issues and turbulence issues at the same time. Heaven knows the bike you're riding was probably delivered to the dealership on a truck, and that's as close to one as it ever needs to be.

COUNTERSTEERING

When I talk countersteering I should let you know that I am not going to talk precession or lean angle or rake or trail or motorcycle dynamics or tire footprint or any kind of calculus. If you want to talk using π to calculate steering geometry and center of mass, go right ahead, because the only pie I'm willing to talk is whether blackberries and marionberries are the same thing. This little piece isn't about math or physics or geometry, it is about saving your life. (Pretentious? Yes. Necessary? Absolutely).

Here's where I'm coming from: Riders tend to fear two kinds of wrecks—getting rear ended and having someone turn left into our paths. Riders do get rear ended and it's a reasonable, but low risk. Left turning drivers are a nuisance, and they kill and injure lots of riders; however, we riders are the single largest danger to ourselves. The real problem is that single vehicle motorcycle accidents are the number one killer of riders. Single rider accidents tend to be "running wide and striking a fixed object." Yeah, you're more likely to crash and kill yourself than to have someone crash into you—*that* is why countersteering is soooo important to know *how* to do.

If you have the conscious ability to countersteer, you have the ability to increase your lean and tighten your line. The mechanizations of steering and lean and precession and center of gravity are really not that important. I have a vague idea of how airplanes fly, I understand lift and thrust, but frankly, I'm not an aerodynamic engineer and don't need to be in order to order a diet soda and enjoy my flight.

What is a countersteer? A countersteer is a press, at speeds greater than twelve miles per hour, on the handlebars on the side of the direction you wish to turn. To be completely simple: Put your hands up in front of you like you're riding your motorcycle. Now, if you want to turn left, press forward with your left hand. This will lean the bike to the left. Do the same to the right, and the bike will lean to the right.

To test this on a ride find a long, straight, deserted road. Be going about 25 or 30 mph. Get in the left lane position. *Gently* press forward on the right grip. The bike will move to the right. Gently press on the left. The bike will move to the left. *That* is a countersteer. It works at speeds greater than 10 to 14 mph. In a turn you can tighten your line by pressing on the inside grip.

That skill, being able to tighten your line with a countersteer, appears to be lacking in many crash-involved motorcyclists. When you see a news story with a line like, "X lost control of his motorcycle causing him to hit the guard rail, leaving the bike and coming to rest in the roadway," or, "X failed to negotiate a turn, left the roadway, and was thrown from his motorcycle," you're probably reading about a rider who didn't know to "press on the inside hand grip to tighten his line."

Often, when riders come into a corner hot they just go wide and "leave the paved roadway." Sometimes they brake, which slows the bike, stands it up and—you guessed it—the bike runs wide and off the road.

Often, riders get caught up in the "have to know how it works" world of physics. I say, if that's your thing, cool, just don't confuse the issue to the point that everyone is so disoriented that they won't try it because there's so much smoke in the room that no one can see the door.

Long ago, when I was in college, a friend and I decided that jumping out of an airplane would be a reasonable and exciting experience. We both knew a guy who had thirty or forty jumps, and he hooked us up with a jumpmaster and a school, where we went out to train and jump. Surprisingly, after only a couple hours we were jump-ready. To be perfectly clear, this was not a tandem jump like you see often today. This was a "static line" jump, a little like you've see John Wayne do, where you clip a line to the plane and then jump out. Only we didn't really have a big plane to work with; in fact, it was a good-sized, over-wing single engine plane. You couldn't stand up in it. The door didn't open, it was simply removed and we all just climbed in and sat on the floor.

About climbing in—it turns out that college students trying to prove their manliness have to jump from 9,000 feet; experienced free-falling folks jump from 13,000 feet. This means that since they are the last out the, 13K crew has to load in first, then the 9K guys hop in. It's classic first in, last out; last in, first out. Pretty simple until two meatheads are standing under the wing trying to figure out who is going to prove their manhood first. It's a lot like your first smoke/drink/breaking-and-entering; you want to let the other guy go first and he wants you to, and then things break down to "paper, rock, scissors." As usual, I was the last to climb in.

Being the first guy out of the plane isn't a really big deal for me; I am thoughtful, but not a thinker. I realize that the physics of jumping are fabulous and interesting but for me my concern is process, not theory. My singular goal once I realize I'm first out the door is simple and vain: I do not want to *fall* out of the plane; I want to do it right—I do not want to trip and take a header out the non-existent door. I know what to do. I've internalized it. I am going to take each step and do each step correctly. The plan, I am sticking to the plan.

The process of a static jump in this situation went like this: The jumpmaster tells me, "Feet out." I swing my feet out over 9,000 feet of nothing and put my right foot on the locked, fixed wheel of the landing gear; my left foot is on the step that is on the strut of the wheel. (See how this can be a little tricky?) Next comes the command, "Climb out," and I reach out, grab the wing strut, and hang off the strut. Yes, you're reading right; I'm hanging off the wing strut of a plane, attached by my own sound grip and a static line that is secured to me and the plane. When I let go of the wing I will arch my back and pray like I really, really mean it.

"GO!!!" yells the jumpmaster. I let go of that perfectly good plane (not that I could have climbed back in), arch my back, and freefall about forty feet before getting a pretty good jerk on the shoulders and compaction of my...package. Looking up I see a wonderfully round, green parachute. Reaching up I find the steering toggles (little wooden handles) and steer right, then left. Things are working nicely. Odd fact: I can actually hear people on the ground talking. I don't know how or why, but I can actually hear people talking to each other several thousand feet below me.

After eavesdropping a moment, I realize that I can now watch my buddy jump from the plane. I look up and start watching the plane circle, waiting to see my friend climb out, hang there, and then drop off the wing. Should be cool, yes? The plane keeps circling, and circling, and circling. No show. No buddy. After a couple of moments, I see him climb out and kinda fall off the plane.

Later, on the ground I asked him what happened and he told me, "The guy told you to put your feet out and you did. He told you to climb out and you did. He told you to go and you were gone. That's when I realized that we were jumping out of an airplane."

I was engaged in process, I was thinking about the little steps, not the big picture; my friend on the other hand suddenly started thinking big picture and when he saw it, he locked up a bit. (They were, apparently, about to pass him over for the other more experienced jumpers so they could ascend to 13,000 feet and jump, when he realized that a great deal of machismo was at stake and he climbed out.)

Jumping out of a sound, airworthy plane is counter-intuitive—it doesn't make sense, but it is worth the reward. Floating around up there is a good time. I did something most people never get the chance to do. I proved I could suppress my fears and trust the training I had received. The equipment worked, the training worked, and I worked. Call it a win.

Is countersteering counter-intuitive? Yes, but if you're riding around turns successfully at speeds greater than 15 mph, then you're already doing it and just don't know it. *Knowing* that a press on the inside grip will tighten your line is a *life saving skill*. Knowing the physics? Fun, confusing, full of argument and intimidation, and generally, talking about it leads to long, confusing, acrimonious debates. When someone wants to go there, I won't go. Why? Because I don't want to get stuck in the plane; I want to jump. I won't have that fight, because I don't need numbers and physics to prove it—doing it proves it. Not a believer? That's OK; try it out in the parking lot. You'll see it works.

Arguing about countersteering only wastes time and energy, knowing how to countersteer and being able and willing to do it *will* save your bacon someday.

PASSING

Can you imagine even asking the question: "How do I make a pass?" The answer is sooo simple! Just like you would in a car: check to see what the oncoming traffic is like, signal your intentions, look over your shoulder (to make sure no one is passing you), and twist the throttle. It's like breathing. How hard can it be? Pretty hard if you've never done it on a bike before because on a bike you're so much more exposed and vulnerable.

The acceleration and power of a motorcycle are a blessing and a curse for you once you decide to pass. First, you usually have an unseemly amount of horsepower at your disposal and good gear selection should put you right on the powerband so you can turn the throttle and go. That same horsepower is also a curse because if you're not judicious in using it you can wind up going 100 or more miles per hour before you realize what you've done.

It's one of those things like being able to eat a lot of food— you get to eat a lot of food but when you're done, dude, you ate a lot of food and may have to pay for it. As with eating, when you're planning a pass the best thing to remember is not to get into a hurry; you want to have a bit of a plan and pace yourself.

Ask yourself this: why do some riders insist on passing cars over the double yellow? The DY (double yellow) is there for a reason. In traffic engineer speak the DY means that there's not enough space for you to cleanly pass. Visibility is probably limited (hill or curve) or there may be an intersection coming up. If you're worried I'm gonna get all preachy here, let me say right off, I am a sinner. I have passed over the double yellow. I even had a phase back in the early '80s when I was absolutely sure that the little strip of pavement between the solid yellow lines was actually a teeny tiny motorcycle lane...I mean, your tire fits it perfect, right? It made perfect sense then, but not so much now.

Due to the acceleration that modern bikes have, there are clearly strips of road where making a pass over the DY is probably possible, but isn't that the same as saying, "Odds are you won't be audited so do what you please on that tax return." When a traffic engineer is designing a road he's working from the lowest common denominator, he's not thinking, "Could a blown 1300cc inline-four motorcycle with a quick shifter make a pass here?" Chances are his calculus car is gonna be something along the lines of your nana's Aries K car. (If you know what that is, welcome to my side of the generation gap.)

When you've got the ponies on hand that we have you should be able to make quick, authoritative passes in situations where they are legally allowed. You should have the time to decide when and how. Once you decide to ignore the double yellow is when the danger really starts. First, no one expects to get passed, and they may be sloppy in their line selection or speed control, and as you pass them the unexpected can happen. Second, because you're operating in close quarters you tend to have to really use the gas to get it done. That sudden burst of acceleration can put you at a speed that makes taking that next corner pretty awkward. (Been there, done that.) Remember, about half of motorcycle fatalities are single vehicle accidents, which means we run off the road and into things. Remember what the racers say, "In slow-out fast. In fast-out dead." Even in a normal, legal situation you need to remember to plan ahead so you don't overcook that turn at the end of the straight. If you're passing in a no passing zone then the situation is amplified and even more dangerous. Which is why you shouldn't pass over the DY.

There's a contractor about thirty-five feet away from me as I write this. He's remodeling and expanding the fabulous Hacienda de la Crash to fit my mother in comfortably. Occasionally he pulls me aside and offers me two options: the "right way" and the "it'll meet code" way. As a bit of a traffic scofflaw, I have always been a bit of a fan of "it'll meet code." My contractor is a fan of the "right way." I am now a much bigger fan of the "right way" because as we've gone along he always explains the advantages and disadvantages of both. There seems to be a rule I've noticed—the right way never has a "but" attached to it; yet, when we talk "meeting code" we end up with a "but..."

One of the calculations that my pop would ask me to do before a big decision was a pro/con or a plus/minus worksheet. You drew a line down the page and you put "pros" on one side and "cons" on the other, then you did the mental calculations to decide whether there were more pros or cons and used that to make the choice. As a young man I would bend the heck out of the pros to make them appear to outweigh the cons. Take, for example, when I bought my first car, which was a 1963 BMW 1600. If you know Beemers, you know the 1600 was the lesser version of the 2002. I was convinced it was a "classic" and Pop new it was an "economy" version, but he let me make up my own calculus and create a world where it was a genius decision—which it wasn't. I figured that out later, standing in a machine shop realizing that selling the long block to the mechanic made more sense than trying to get it sleeved and the valves ground.

Let's do the pro/con math you should do before you go to pull a pass.

Pro: Passing will get you back up to speed, and conserve time.

Pro: Passing will get you around and give you a better field of vision. (Slowing and increasing your following distance will do the same).

Pro: Ahh...let me think...OH! Passing will get you out of the trail of carbon monoxide and particulate yuck that the car in front of you is spewing!

Con: Passing could put you in conflict with other users going the other way.

Con: Passing could mean that you're simply exchanging one problem for another. You pass this guy and then you're stuck behind the next guy.

Con: Passing could mean robustly violating the speed limit. Check your state for rules, but some state code I've seen says you don't get to speed to pass—then you're just speeding *and* passing. Seriously, look it up. See if it says, "Yup you may do the ton to slap a pass on a Prius."

Like a lot of things, passing can show a lot of negatives, which is why you want to be careful slapping a pass on someone. Remember my contractor? Think "meet code." You can make a pass here...*but*...

My two cents: If you're gonna make a pass, be sure you can make it quick, clean, and in a legal area. I am really smitten with slow traffic turnouts and short "Keep Right Except to Pass" sections of road. People expect to pass and be passed there, so they are excellent places to do it. The guy who designed the road actually made those spots for guys like you and me who need to get around someone once in a while. As far as the double yellow goes, that's not there to make your life difficult, it's there to extend your life. Short of an emergency evasion, I can't think of any reason to cross over it anymore. But that's just this old sinner's opinion. Now, I like doing it right.

WAX ON, WAX OFF

No we're not talking paint or polish, or karate; we're talking the idea of "waxing and waning," which is the idea that things increase (wax) and then decrease (wane) often in a natural cycle. The Moon, that huge chunk of rock that orbits our planet, waxes full and then wanes, growing full, then fading and then growing full again. That is the kind of waxing and waning I want to talk about. During our lives we all wax and wane; education waxes as we go through school and then may wane as we get career interested and we focus our learning on our professions; our general education wanes and our professional education waxes. Wait, I have a good example—my pop and ice cream.

Pop was an engineer and about the time I was ten or twelve years old he took up a real love of making ice cream. I remember he would have us hand crank the ice cream out on the deck of a house we lived in—he had done extensive remodeling and we were out on a big redwood deck he had designed and built. We cranked a lot of ice cream. My father had learned enough about ice cream to know that at the end of the process, as it stiffens, you really want to beat air into the stuff. It's called "overrun" and is a percentage measure of how much air you beat into an ice cream mix. His theory was that electric freezers slowed at the end, but teenage freezers could crank hard, get tired, and hand off and keep up the overrun. Eventually Pop created a formula for ice cream, he knew all about cream and milk fat and what he wanted the ice cream to do.

Yup, it was like that, he knew where to tweak what to get a texture or overrun he wanted. We cranked ice cream for church socials, birthdays, business luncheons, I believe even a wedding or two; he was well-known for his ice cream making prowess. I cannot put the mental picture into your mind of his ability to dissect ice cream—he used an early Hewlett-Packard computer at work to create formulas and check ratios and learn how ice cream worked. I know about how ice cream matures and oxidizes because of all this research and Pop's pool of knowledge.

Eventually, he moved into experiments with sherbets and sorbets, but then his interest had waxed as full as it could and then waned. Waning isn't the end of something. It's the settling of something, the movement from the fore to the foundation. Ice cream did not disappear from Pop's life; it simply wasn't the center anymore. That is waning, the idea that something doesn't leave you, it simply moves from center stage to the wings, it goes from sun to moon, always there, just not as bright. We moved from always hand cranking to using an electric machine. (Granted, there was only one kind that was good enough for the job.) The ice cream autopsy ended. We simply ate it and enjoyed it. Though the focus was still to make great ice cream, we moved to a phase where an accomplished artisan worked his craft without the mandate to forever break it down and make it better.

In his ice cream career my dad reached his point of equilibrium. What happened? I think I know—because the same thing happens to me with my writing; I wax and I wane. In all things we wax and wane. Right now I'm cranking out 1,000 to 3,000 words a day on this very book. I went through a stint were I couldn't get a 1,000 words in a week. My focus was elsewhere—I can write, but there are other things that come to the fore and grab the spotlight and demand to be dealt with. Slowly it becomes easy to put it off, to do it occasionally. There's not the drive, the need, the demand to write. Now, as things have slowed down, there are all these things that need to pour out of me and I'm writing, editing, organizing, and constantly reviewing. Right now I'm waxing, and as I wax I am enjoying the process; it's pleasant and enjoyable, and I look forward to it. Part of my process is tuning and toning what I write. I see a lot of my father in me when I'm this focused.

Your riding career will have waxing and waning moments. Why? Because that's the nature of a lot of things in life. You get crazy focused in love and later it does one of two things; it either grows into something different and more mature, or it burns out and fades away. Are there different variations of waning? Is it a scale? I would say yes. I get paid to instruct new riders. That makes me a "safety professional" and guess what? Sometimes I don't look forward to teaching. I simply go and do it. I am waned. Other times I'm nuts for the stuff. I wake up three hours early. I go and set the range up before the other instructor has eaten his breakfast. I am waxed, focused, into it, all in, and just love the devil out of it and teach ten to fifteen cycles of training. Come back a year later and I'm only gonna teach three—because I've waned.

During your riding career you might even go through a time when you don't ride…and that's OK, because everyone waxes and wanes.

Keep Riding or
Start Crashing?

Here's an idea I've shared before: Motorcycles, at speed, like to run straight and true, guided by the same basic principles that (in sixth grade) allowed you to take a "borrowed" Stingray bicycle and launch it for a "ghost ride." Motorcycles carrying any speed, unless they are in some way gravely wounded, will stand up and run straight. (Why do you think you have to steer them to turn—by nature they want to run in a straight line.) This tiny bit of insight is crucial to my strategy of what to do when things go wrong. I believe that if you can get the idea that bikes naturally want to run straight and true, you have taken the first step to being immunized to crashing. Here's why: Running wide is the bike's way of doing its natural thing, trying to run straight and true—so you need to steer. Likewise, if you're riding down the road and something deflects the front tire, the bike wants to go straight and true—which means that as long as you don't make some impulsive, insane braking or steering input the bike is going to continue straight and true.

To be succinct, if things get weird, often the best thing to do is nothing.

Ever heard that dude with the well-worn leather jacket say, "Chop it and drop it"? That's old-school, good-old-boy for the idea that if you're in a tight spot and the bike starts to quiver or slip, stay on the gas. See this is another way of saying sometimes the best thing to do is nothing. When old school chopper vets say, "Don't touch the front brake or you'll crash," they're actually saying, "The best thing to do is nothing." How do I figure? Because both those actions—chopping the throttle or hammering the brake—can create a massive traction consuming input. Think about it a moment. You're on the road, in a turn, you hit a small rock or a patch of sand, and the front tire slips or deflects slightly. What does that tire want to do? Keep on keeping on. But you, now freaked because something just happened, instantly decide you should do something and grab the binders, or make a big steering input, and suddenly a wheel or bike that's trying to return to path or regain composure is yammed off its line, and things can get fugly fast. In other words, instead of simply riding our bikes and letting them do what they want to do, we actively crash them.

I now sing praises to "pausing a second." Pausing a second when your wife asks, "How do you like the new hair color?" is a good idea. Pausing a second when the boss says, "You wouldn't mind working this weekend, would you?" is a good idea. Pausing a second when your child points at your gut and asks, "Daddy, are you gonna have a baby, too?" is—you're right—a good idea. I often tell people that the toughest trick to learn is "biting your tongue." Being able to not speak your mind is an invaluable skill. Due to the number of times I've had a polite smile on my face whilst screaming in my head, "Are you a complete idiot!? That's the stupidest ****ing thing I've ever heard a human being say!" I won't bother regaling you with tales of the dumb things I have let bounce off my forehead. Suffice it to say that by being able to pause and not say a thing I have saved my marriage, job, and life several dozen times by simply doing and saying nothing.

Here's what happens with bikes: We get our minds all wrapped up in the idea that our skills, our sharpened, ready for action in the middle of the night, can disembowel you with a spoon or turn strawberry jell-o into napalm skills will get us out of any bind we can get ourselves into, and we need to be ready at any second to use them. We are so hyper-prepared to do something, at anytime, anywhere, that we are primed to kill, prepared to act, itching for action and when something happens that requires we do nothing we often do something we shouldn't.

"Chop it and drop it" is an excellent example of the need to pause and do nothing. Sportbike riders really suffer from this problem; they are worried about spinning up the rear end and low-siding. The average (and probably even above average) sport rider, will never be in a situation where he's going to tear the rear wheel loose with the throttle exiting a turn. Yet, in the rush of, "Man, I'm really getting it done," he may find himself in a place where the back does step out due to surface imperfection or some foreign object on the road. In that instant, when the back end quivers and is unsettled, if he suddenly chops the throttle, he dramatically changes the weight bias of the bike, putting weight on the front and taking it off the rear. The bike, now unsettled and victim of a dramatic control input can react poorly. The front, which may have been consuming nearly 100% of available traction, suddenly needs 110%, and he tucks the front. BOOM! He's on the ground. Or the rear, which would have recovered smoothly if he had simply kept a even throttle, will violently regain traction and potentially high-side him.

Can you survive "chopping it"? Yes. You can. I have...by the skin of my teeth. I've chopped it when I shouldn't have and had the back snap back into line so violently that it nearly bucked me off MotoGP style. There's a good idea there— watch some motorcycle racing sometime and watch how the rider responds to trouble. Keep a keen eye on a bike that's being raced; it's a quivering, flexing, wobbling mess. Under braking, the front is buried and the back is in the air and wriggling. On the gas the front is in the air and the back is slithering back and forth. It's just a fiesta of flexibility, a circus of squirm, a ballet of balance! If you're convinced that high intensity cornering should be "planted" and "on rails" you're right—if you're riding a street bike at reasonable speeds. But there is a twist. When a bike stops feeling that way, it doesn't mean that a crash is imminent, it may simply be the bike wandering out towards its boundaries, getting close to the edge of the envelope, and behaving like it. This is the part where you need to think a moment, because if you're moving out toward the edge of the performance envelope, how much room do you have left for mistakes? And how quickly can you get in real trouble if you make a sudden, large, traction-consuming input?

This is all working its way to a "take it to the track" piece, and if that's what you are getting from it that's great, but I think there's more to this discussion than just "go to the track." Even in normal riding there are situations where the bike is near the edge of its performance envelope, and you can crash yourself with an input that startles the bike. Remember how you don't like surprises? "Honey—good news—my mother is moving in with us!" Yeah..."Good news! I've just violently overspent the available traction by whacking on the front brake!" Same exact thing. Right after that, everybody's on the floor wondering what the flipping flapjacks just happened.

Please do not read this as a endorsement to crash. Be willing and ready to control your motorcycle. If you're running wide, brakes probably aren't the answer, but a gentle press on the inside grip will tighten your line and get you around the turn. There will be times when your bike speaks to you and needs an immediate reaction from you—but there are others when the bike is gonna grunt or squirm and it's just telling you, "We're getting a little out there," and it doesn't need or want you to do anything except keep riding it. Please, be careful not to misread what your bike is saying to you. Here's a mother-in-law of an idea: If your wife tells you her mom is visiting for a few days should you react like you just got told she's moving in?

REMOUNTING

Theoretically, I should do that "get back on the horse" thing, but we're riders, here, so let's talk about remounting. You can't remount until you demount. Crap, this is sounding silly. Let me tell you a story and see if we can't avoid the horses and instead talk bikes.

Early today I was the "B" instructor at a basic rider training course. In this class we had three or four actual "never been on a bike before" riders. Yeah, it is a beginner's course, but we get a lot of folks with a fair amount of experience. So, as a coach, when you get a true. complete newb you get your radar set on high and try to take care of them. To the point, I had a nice twenty something young lady who was riding a motorcycle for the very first time, and she was alternately doing well and suffering minor setbacks. Occasionally, she would do things like drop the clutch on starting out and stall, then get going and recover, and then go out and really do well on an exercise. She was hit and miss, but overall going the right way.

Since it was the second day of training we get to "Stopping Quickly" (emergency stops). I'm a little nervous because if a new rider's head is not in the game he can end up locking the front, and if he doesn't let it go and reapply, he can end up on the deck. Asking a truly newb rider to come down the chute at 20 mph and trying to coach them to getting stopped in 23 feet can be a bit nerve racking for all involved.

When I speak of a braking chute, I'm talking about an imaginary rectangular box. Riders start about 150 feet away, catch second gear, and for the first few attempts enter the short side of the box, marked by an eighteen inch cone at 15 mph. As they pass the cone they squeeze the clutch, downshift and apply both brakes simultaneously, and then stop in the shortest possible safe distance. After they've landed, a coach (me) walks up and gives them praise and coaching. After a few runs at 15 mph, we bump them up to 20 and things can get kinda interesting.

As an instructor you really do worry about your students. Motorcycling is a dangerous business, and most coaches are looking to share knowledge and help people have more enjoyable, less risky riding careers. More often than not we're pretty dang excited to see you making good progress and having a good time. In the pantheon of things we say—which is everything from "Head and eyes up!" to "Progressively squeeze on the brake; don't grab!"—my favorite command is, "It's OK to smile!"

Riders in training should be having moments when they are having a good time. They need to have success and enjoy success. On the flip side is the fact that things can go wrong in training. Good Lord, it is motorcycle training; you're doing something risky; you signed a waiver in case you die; its people and machines and there is the possibility of disaster. (In my world that makes things fun.) In the real world it means that a rider can get into a vicious cycle of defeatism that can destroy self-confidence and create a situation in which learning is impossible. Once a student, no matter how motivated, decides he can't do it, that it's too dangerous; he can't. In anything you attempt you can be your worst enemy. No one on earth can break your spirit as quickly as you can.

As my slowly improving young lady was at the staging cone (first in line), I took a deep breath and gave her the signal to proceed down to the braking chute at 20 mph. As an instructor I know I am upping the stakes, things are going from falling at 15 to potentially falling at 20. I was confident that if she simply kept doing what she was doing she was going to be OK. I've had folks tuck the front and drop the bike before; it's unsettling but extremely survivable and usually results in nothing more serious than a bruised ego. Bumping her up to 20 put me on edge. I'm sure it put her on edge too...well, I'm sure it did because of what transpired next.

At the braking cone our heroine grabbed a massive handful of front brake. This resulted in the front wheel locking and then, well, things got truly weird. Remember, when you've think you've seen it all that's when the powers that be decide to remind you that ya haven't. The appropriate reaction to a locked front is to keep the bars straight and release the brake. Unfortunately, our girl started to turn the bars with the front wheel still locked. She started to turn and I thought, "Here we go, gonna tuck the front," because I've seen it before and was figuring on seeing it again. Cue fate. With the bike on the way down, she released the front brake and whacked the throttle wide open. The bike, now under power, snapped upright and started running for the fence about fifty feet away. Seeing the fence our rider *let go* of the handlebars and (I thought) was going to roll off the back of the bike. My mind was all ready to see her roll off the back, and the bike ghost ride into a curb and a chain-link fence.

I was positive that was what I was seeing! With her legs locked straight out at the knees, I swear this is true, her feet were above the bars, her hands splayed out over her shins. She had rolled backward, the small of her back was on the passenger seat, and I was writing the report in my mind. Cue fate again. Without input the throttle closed, the bike slowed, and our rider rolled back down, put both feet on the pegs, both hands on the handlebars, grabbed a big handful of brake, locked the front, turned the bars right, and tucked the front, falling to the right. It was truly impressive. It was acrobatic, heart stopping, with unexpected twists and turns, but delivering what you'd expect in the end. It would have been a perfect summer movie.

Once a rider falls I have a nasty habit: I don't run to them. I'll walk with determination or jog with purpose, but I don't throw a clipboard up in the air and start running unless you're on fire, pinned under a running bike, or there's visible bone and arterial blood flow—none of which I've ever seen. If you're thirty feet away standing next to a bike on its side, I'll briskly walk to you and assess the situation, then take action. I don't run because I have kids, and I've learned over the years that if a kid isn't hurt and you scream, "OH MY GOD!" and run over, it takes what's a mild situation and amps it up. Likewise, if it is serious you can settle it down by being calm.

When I get there our rider is just about to try to pick the bike up. I told her not to bother, that I would. The deal I made was simple: "I'll get the bike up, and while I do that, take physical stock and make sure you're OK." As a system it ain't perfect but if someone is hurt and doesn't realize it yet I don't want them aggravating an injury trying to pick a bike up. The bike came back up, our girl took off a glove to inspect the heel of one hand (no damage), and within two minutes we were at the threshold of a very difficult conversation—the "Are you ready to remount?" conversation.

When a rider in training falls two things happen; first, it can physically or mentally break the student, and second, if the student who falls is seriously broken he can mentally take other riders with him. It is best for everyone if, short of physical injury, the rider who falls can get back up and remount. I'm not talking about bullying people back onto a bike who shouldn't be riding. I'm talking about people who are looking seriously at riding, and seeing a glimpse of the potential reality, they get jittery and make a bad decision based on adrenaline and wounded pride.

After the obligatory "Do you want medical attention?" I always ask, "So, where you at? You want to take a breath and get back after it?" Offering a chance to pause seems to me to be the way to go. I'm not gonna just up and say, "You in or out?" The situation isn't that complex, but it's not that simple either—think of it as a kid getting bit by the puppy they've always wanted and you're in the 'hood. You get training to learn to do something and sometimes you learn things you didn't expect to or don't want to know.

Here's why, at the end of the day, I told this young lady she was my hero. When I asked her what she wanted to do she said, "I want to take a moment and stop shaking. I don't want to quit because I want to prove I can do this...I don't want to give up and then regret it. I don't want it to beat me." We waited a moment, she remounted, the bike fired right up, and after taking a deep breath, she looked at me and I asked, "You ready?" She said, "Yes." And back up the center of the range she went, made a U-turn, lined up, and we started work on "Stopping Quickly" again.

Riding is an intensely personal business. We all ride for differing reasons, but one of the most common threads is the ability to control our own environment and how we interact with it. Being "in charge" on a bike, exposed to element and accident, knowing that we ultimately make our own decisions, is a part of the motorcycling psyche. We ride because we want to. Nothing is more heroic to me, or deserves more praise than when someone gets knocked down, gets up, and then remounts—and not out of embarrassment, but out of a conscious decision to better themselves. Did our young hero pass? I'm not supposed to tell you those sorts of things, and I'm going to keep my honor intact and not tell you if she did or did not meet program standard—but I will say this: In my book? Hero, no questions asked, no more proving to be done.

THE ILLUSION OF SPEED

There's no nice way to say this, but there are those who, once they read this, will tell you to never read a word of what I write again. I can't help them out, this is a serious topic and one befuddling enough that some people will tell you that we should never speak of it. If you are that sort, if you're not a hooligan, if you're easily offended when others bruise the motor vehicle code, then you need to turn away because here's the dealio: Once you've been running 120 mph for a while, chugging along at 55 seems kinda slow. There. I said it. I have played fast and loose with the speed limit. Well, maybe more than fast and loose. Maybe I pillaged and looted it a little too... hard to say. Clearly I was disrespectful. OK, OK, I took it to the prom, liquored it up, brought it home two days later missing a slipper, and never called back. I'm a bad man. I'm also not the pope or the president. I am indeed human, and I, like many other human beings, find speed thrilling and fascinating. Going fast in a straight or curved line excites me.

In motorsports you'll hear about "speed junkies," which is a term used to describe people who enjoy going fast. I believe there is a difference between speed junkies and pudding-for-brains people who just routinely speed. Routine speeders are a dangerous lot. They simply drive everywhere too fast. Routine speeders are involved in single car accidents and cause multiple car accidents. A routine speeder is a person who generally doesn't realize he is speeding, or when caught, gets huffy about the "injustice" and "oppressive nature" of traffic laws.

Speed junkies don't get caught—and when they do they're interested in getting radar verification of their speed. See, a speed junkie isn't the sort who runs down to the store and does 55 in a 25 school zone while dodging nuns and orphans in the crosswalk. Speed junkies will look around and find an appropriate place to do their thing. The word *junkie* implies a person who is hooked, but you have to remember that a person who is hooked is also careful—tends to hide his habit—he doesn't snort or shoot his junk in the baby aisle at the department store. Junkies are a secretive lot. Absolutely we have junkies who are strung out and on the corner, messed up and obvious, but you may not realize the number of junkies there are out there, because a good junkie is good at hiding his habit. Speed junkies are the same; it isn't until they are in the throes of self-destruction that they start dragging two lane suburban streets.

A motorcycle speed junkie is an interesting thing because at some level, like all junkies, he realizes he has a problem. For me? There's a county next door that has more cows than people, where the stimulus bill has paid for some really nice new highway, and where there is only one deputy on duty at any given time—that's either a problem or a blessing for me. Yeah, if you're a speed junkie you know that sort of thing. It's the place I go to do the stupid stuff, and at some point out there you realize that, yup, it's pretty stupid what you're doing. You come to understand you've got a problem. It's tough realizing that you're running your life in a manner that can harm you; it takes some getting used to. By this I mean if you're a person who knows what a good sized motorcycle running in sixth gear at 8 or 9k sounds like, then you're probably on the verge of enlightenment.

Heading out to that empty space and letting a bike really run is a good sign that you might have issues. I'm not talking about tapping the ton and running back down (going 100 mph for four seconds). I'm talking about seeing speeds well above 100 for sustained periods of time. I'm talking about running a bike hard, not about being "speed-curious," but about actively trying to top the bike out—and staying there. This is about being in that place long enough to seriously start thinking thoughts like,

"I wonder if the guy who made these tires was really paying attention to the process..."

"If I hit a rabbit at this speed, the best course of action is no action...it should just disintegrate...Force equals mass times acceleration squared right?"

"That isn't a turn up there, that's a bend...so...do I really need to brake?"

"Man, going 55 feels like I'm going backwards—I think I could run this fast!"

Yup, one of the illusions of speed is that you're not going that fast—I mean once you've gone that fast and then slow down, it seems like you're not moving. For me, when I was looking around thinking, "Boy, I'm gonna get rear-ended if I don't pick it back up. Running 25 mph on a two lane state highway is a bad idea," only to look down to see 55 mph on the clocks was a "oh shizz" moment. It leads to things like finally realizing that if you crash out here in the boonies with no one around, they might not find your bike or body until the vultures are circling. Even that's not a sure thing, because there are more cows than people in this county by a long shot, and dead cows ain't that unique.

The illusion of speed is that you can become immune to it. You've gone really, really fast and suddenly normal fast isn't fast anymore, and you lose your respect for 35 or 45 or 55 mph, any of which could easily provide you with sudden, certain, violent death. I imagine it's the same for any drug.

You can be a functioning speed junkie—you can hide it, indulge it, keep it to yourself, and nobody will ever know. But being a motorcycle speed junkie is every bit a dangerous habit because once a little isn't enough and you need more, things can get out of hand easily. When going 85 seems slow you've got a problem. You can ride way, way too fast out in the boonies on a regular basis and survive—there's lots of living proof walking around right now. A careful dose of horsepower in the right place at that right time can be copious fun; the problem isn't picking the right time or place, the problem is you'll never be sure when the wrong time or place might happen. Big speed on the street carries with it big risks that you can't control—things like basic bike maintenance; your bike may be a race replica but have you maintained it to race standards? What about wildlife? My state is an open range state and that means don't be surprised to see cows *on the road*. What about other users? What about things other users deposit on the road surface? You may have V rated tires (150 mph) on a Z rated bike (capable of over 150 mph). Ever had an engine stumble at speed? How 'bout a speed wobble?—is that steering damper new and adjusted correctly?

If you want to do big speed, do it in the right place, a track. Tracks have tech inspections, run out if you go wide, emergency medical aid on site, schools, instructors, and insurance. Just because you survive your weekly kamikaze runs out in the desert doesn't mean they're safe—it means you're a good planner and have some luck kicked in by fate. A coyote crossing a highway at a trot may not be really good for a bike going 255 feet per second, which is a very doable speed on lots of bikes.

Another illusion of speed is that you're the only one at risk. You're not. Other users are at risk. You can carry enough energy with a speeding bike to kill just about everybody in a small car. What about your family and friends? You may not be your biggest fan, but I bet your momma or spouse or significant other thinks pretty dang highly of you and would prefer you remain as physically and mentally sound as you are right now.

The illusion of speed cuts both ways, and that's what makes it tricky to discuss with riders. There's a fine line in the discussion that we as riders and the general public have a tough time nuancing.

Speed can kill—but there's no guarantee it will.

See that? I've folded, spindled, and mutilated the speed limit, and the two times I've been on the pavement on the road I was going the speed limit. Speed? I got away with it...still do in fact! How do you reconcile that? In a society enamored with absolutes, people want to say, "Every single person who speeds and rides like an idiot dies," so how does a guy like me say, "It didn't kill me, not even a scratch." Am I nuts? Heretical? Honest? How does speed kill and guys like me survive?

The illusion runs both ways. Those who speed will convince themselves they can't be hurt; those that don't speed will convince themselves it's an unsurvivable event. The illusion is in the disconnect we as riders have—we tend to fall on one side or the other instead of being honest and standing in the middle. Yeah, the middle. If you're cursing the page right now saying, *"I never speed,"* I appreciate your lying nature because, my brother or sister—you do. *All* have sinned and fallen short. It may have been in the minivan trying to get your kid to clarinet practice on time, and it may have been inadvertent, but you did it and you know it.

You have broken the speed limit, by omission or commission, and speeding didn't kill you, but the illusion tricks your mind here as well! Just because speeding didn't kill you doesn't mean it can't kill you, or it hasn't killed others. The beautiful mirage of talking about speeding is that it's whatever you want it to be. It's the perfect chameleon; it disguises itself to fight your mind and my mind differently at the same time.

In the end, speeding is illegal. If you get caught, expect to be fined. It is dangerous because it places you in a situation where you're not behaving as those around you are and expect you to. Speed limits are designed to help keep the lowest common denominator safe. Speeding can be illusionary—what you see as safe, prudent, and reasonable others may see as reckless, immature, and dangerous. Am I gonna say, "Go out there and go, Bunky, go; speed like you mean it, it's all good!" No. I am not. But I do understand that it happens, and I pray whether you're speeding by design or by oversight, nothing bad happens to you.

THE DEATH GRIP

Ever get back from a ride and have to peel your fingers off the grips? You know, walk around with your hands in an arthritic-looking curl? Or perhaps you've awakened the morning after and your forearms are cramped or your fingers are stiff. These are signs that instead of riding your bike, you're trying to choke it to death. The "death grip" is a symptom. If you find yourself trying to crush your handlebar in your hands it usually means one thing, you are in the early stages of "freaked out." Here's what you need to do: figure out why you're starting to freak out. Remember how it is always better to catch a cancer early on? Before it can grow and spread? Yea, an ounce of prevention is worth a pound of cure.

A rider with a death grip on the bars is a rider who has started down a dangerous and volatile path that can lead to an accident report with quotes like, "The bike wouldn't turn" or, "There was nothing I could do; the bike just wouldn't respond." Why does that happen? Well, first, you're choking the grips, then your arms get tight and your inputs are no longer fluid, next comes a tight torso, locked shoulders, and a potential to be caught in a shallow breathing cycle (yea, panting a little), which can lead to hyperventilation or oxygen deprivation. You're now impaired, tight as a drum, and trying to operate a bike—that should sound like a recipe for trouble to you. Your breathing and your grip on the bars are excellent indicators of what your mental state is. An overloaded rider is a nervous rider and once you're getting freaked out, those crisp, shallow breaths may be taking in too much or too little oxygen, and you can end up hyperventilated and freaked out in the middle of a turn.

The problem can be a processing one. Generally, a rider who is getting tense is a rider who is overloaded—a reactive rider, instead of a proactive rider. Great riders are not *in* the moment, they are *in front* of the moment. Once you're behind the cascade, and when things are happening to you at a pace you can't process, then you're in serious, deadly trouble. You are no longer in control of events; events are in control of you. That's not to say that you can't ride down the road fat, dumb, and happy as a reactive rider, simply staring at the license plate in front of you like a cow going to the slaughter. The idea that you're nervous is actually a good sign. It means you understand that you're in a risk-filled environment. A rider who is nervous is a rider who is not complacent, but a rider on edge understands he is in a risk-filled environment and that he is just getting left behind, and panic can start as he struggles to keep up.

White knuckles aren't a bad thing, but they are a symptom that you shouldn't ignore. Rule of thumb: If you're squeezing the bars too hard then feel free to pull over and have a conversation with yourself. Ask, "Self, we've been together a long time—whatcha so tense about?" The answer could be you're all freaked out because you were surfing the web at work and found a picture of your boss in a bikini...and he didn't look good at all. (Or maybe he did, and now you're all confused.) Either way, you've got a big chunk of your computing power grinding away about a teensy weensy yellow polka dot bikini when you should be scanning fourteen to twenty-four seconds ahead and coming up with survival strategies and clear pathways. When riding a motorcycle you should be thinking about things like space cushion and path of travel, not your boss's odd...shaving and waxing habits.

If you're not focused on the ride it's OK to stop and get a game reset. I'm always happy when a rider says, "I get nervous and worried out there." I like it because it implies that he understands he is out there where, if things go wrong, he can get squished by vehicles that weigh two to forty tons. Rolling down the highway you should be alert, aware, and maybe a bit alarmed, but there are problems that come when that awareness manifests itself physically. Yes, a tense rider can overreact to the situation. Yes, being tense while having to execute an emergency maneuver can make things a whole heckuva lot worse. And, yes, you should have a finger on the trigger, but it shouldn't be a twitchy one.

You got kids? You got kids in your family? Nieces? Nephews? Go to the second grade play. Spot the nervous kids—yeah the ones that freeze, can't move, can't speak, scared to death. Or the ones that say his their lines too soon and then too loud as well. Or the ones that once they start, they stop—they were doing great—but suddenly self doubt hits them. They think they are doing it wrong, and they restart... and stop...and restart. Listen to the "squeakers" in the band. The clarinets that practiced all week, and now with a death grip on their instruments, they squeak them things like mice in a wringer. Flutists fowl it up too—you'll hear.

If you really want to see how nerves can affect response, causing too much, too soon, too bad, try training people to stop their motorcycles. If you've been through rider training you may have noted that we drill "cover the clutch" into your head. On the range, at all times, trainees are to cover the clutch, but not the brakes. Why? Because covering the levers puts you in ready position, your finger is literally on the trigger, and something as simple as a coach waving to a comrade will trigger a startle reaction and WHAM, your ready-to-contract hand does, in come the levers, and... Jerking a big handful of clutch won't do any damage, but jamming the brake lever to the bar can be a disaster. The extra half second it takes to put your fingers on the brake lever is enough time to realize you don't want to squeeze—Crash is just waving to his family as they arrive with a sandwich and several small dogs.

Say it with me: Nervous is bad. Awareness of the gravity of the situation is good. Aware good; nervous bad. Does that mean you can't be nervous? Heck no. Be nervous, be worried, puke a little in your mouth once in a while, but do not let it get the upper hand. I am aware there is a school of thought out there that says you should "ride like they're all trying to kill you," which is fine, a tad paranoid but you should be watching other users—getting a driver's license is awful easy. Emphasis on *awful*. Folks can whine about how "easy" a motorcycle license is but, dude, really? You can be blind in one eye, have vertigo, three differing types of epilepsy and they are still gonna let you drive a car. So riding with a little awareness that them things might be a little wobbly ain't a bad idea—just don't take it too far. (You know, complaining that a car, innocently drifting in its lane, is trying to run you off the road. If you've ever had a car come after you—by mistake or design—then you'll understand that when they're coming after you—they're coming after you.)

A mindset that is constantly over reaching with the dangers of a situation can place you in that position where you're hyperaware and overly ready to act. Remember, sometimes the best reaction is to do nothing; things will sort themselves out. By getting into an over-revved state of hyper-vigilance you react too quickly, potentially improperly, and can make an innocent situation into a crash. To my mind that rank, frightened reaction of just clenching your fists in panic should be avoided. In the learning environment, it's accomplished by not covering the brake; on the road, it's accomplished by being level-headed and completely alert.

Keeping calm while remaining vigilant isn't impossible—it's a bit like when you're running "a little" over the speed limit—it requires some self-awareness and self-control or "a little" can become a lot. Remember, the slide into impairment is dangerous because it happens without our knowing, a gradual decline in cognitive ability, resulting in an state where, unaware of our impairment, we're at tremendous risk. Here's the dealio: tension, fear, parking it on the edge of panic is a bad scene as well. Be aware, be alert, but don't be freaked out. If you feel like you're getting freaked out then stop, take a few deep breaths, make an accounting of what you're doing and why you're not on your game. Why? Because if you're off your game—it's easy to end up off your bike.

Should have called this the "Kung Fu Grip" but there are probably copyright implications.

PULLING A "RUNNER"

One of the hypothetical questions that people like to bat around when you're telling riding stories and lies is: "Would you ever run from the police?" You're sitting in the backyard, maybe at a friend's BBQ, and younger people will start asking questions like that. Why? I don't know; maybe they're testing the edges to see how you'll respond to the idea of wanton felonious behavior. This is, in my experience, a fairly common question among younger, newer riders. Perhaps it's because they scent the powerful acceleration edge modern bikes have, or maybe they're just speed-curious. They ask and I answer like this.

Back in the day I pulled a runner several times. I never ran to "stick it to The Man" or because I was protecting Tom Jefferson and the Bill of (Speeding) Rights. I ran because I didn't want to pay the ticket or have my insurance rates go up. I share this not to encourage running but to give some insight into when, where, why, and how I ran. I'm assuming that the statute of limitations has lapsed on anything I did back in the early '80s, and if it hasn't then...well...I won't name jurisdictions.

A couple of thoughts right off the top: I ran because I had broken the law *and* I knew it *and* I had done it (never intentionally) in plain view of a police officer. Let me say that when you put the front wheel back on the ground and you're staring a Dodge Polaris in the face, and the officer has already turned on his lights; if you're eighteen, pulling over and taking your medicine just doesn't seem like a good idea. The brain doesn't mature until around twenty-five or twenty-seven years old (coincidentally you get a major insurance break about that age), and at eighteen to twenty years you have a very hard time modeling the future more than thirty days in advance— which means the idea of long term consequence is hard to grasp. Knowing that physiology will help you understand why, when you're young, pulling a runner can *seem* like a good idea.

It's fun as well, because you're young and stupid, and you can't possibly understand the ramifications of things going the wrong way. To use a phrase one of my sons coined when hitting zero Gs and floating in his booster seat as we hustled an SUV over a nifty hilltop, running from the cops will "make your peepee tickle." It's exactly the same as the first time you were with a young lady and put your hand in a forbidden place (and the second time as well). Some things are always thrilling and make your heart pound because you don't know what the outcome is going to be. The rewards could be glorious, the risk immense, and as a teen you can't really understand what actually might happen next (slapped, arrested, shot by officer/ father). You only know that if it goes wrong it will be bad. The impossibility of the "getting it," of the young mind truly understanding the dangers, is what makes running possible and, yes, thrilling. Escape and survive is primordially simple and seen in nature billions of times a day. Pursuit is the ultimate in deathsport. When a young dude decides to run he is, in essence, banking his life on escape; of course his peepee is gonna tickle.

Given the situation when I ran I had one goal: break the line of sight and go to ground as quickly as possible. Somewhere in the last decade or two the idea of the prolonged, county-to-county, state-to-state chase has entered the youth culture. Telegraph from "Back in the Day": The longer you run the more likely you are to be caught. A speeding bike is a high profile bike. "In the day" our theory was break the line of sight, then either hide or simply blend back in—meaning possibly reversing course with heavy traffic and doing nothing to stand out. Once you broke visual contact, you looked to blend back in. There were no cop chase shows or instant "eye in the sky" breaking news, and your goal was to simply vanish.

One runner I pulled happened on a popular road for motorcycling on the weekends. I was running at extra legal speeds, came around a corner, and found myself staring straight into the grill of a police cruiser parked facing me with the radar gun on the dash like some goofy bullhorn. Rolling off the throttle, I popped up out of my (snicker a little here) "racing crouch" and looked down at the clocks—I was doing 80 in a 55. I looked over my shoulder and I saw nothing but a cloud of dust, as this officer clearly was doing a Dukes of Hazard stomp-and-go, trying to get turned around in the gravel and crap on the side of the road where he was parked.

This brings me to a couple of things that were important back then. The first was speed deficit. How big a hole is that cop in? Is he going 65 mph the other way? Or right behind you going the same speed? Or is he stopped? If stopped, does he have to make a U-turn? This poor guy was facing the wrong way, I was going 80 mph, and he still had get that wallowing Polaris turned and that was gonna probably be a three pointer. Really, at nineteen is there any question of what I was gonna do? The bike was piped and jetted, I was running an R compound tire on the front, and I was just the shizz so I didn't slow down. I poured on the coal. I had recognized the car and its jurisdiction, so at the next major road I turned away from his backyard and into the next county, figuring up in the hills where we were that the radio comms couldn't keep up with me.

By turning away from this officer's jurisdiction, I was doing a couple things: I tried to exploit the problem of radio communications, and I also turned down a road that wasn't in his jurisdiction. Why was that important to me? Because I knew the road I was going down very well, and he probably didn't. In any situation you want to ask: Who owns the battlefield? Am I in my own neighborhood or one that I am intimately familiar with? *Or* is this the cop's town? How big a force does that town have? Is it two cars or twenty? Was the officer able to read my tags? Because if they get your tag, they're gonna go wait at your house. Does the CHP or county sheriff patrol there as well—remembering, of course, that *nobody* is as fast as Motorola.

See, if you asked me if I would pull a runner today, I would offer a couple points:

1. GPS—Cops have much more at their disposal than their memories now. The can readily position themselves to cut off fleeing vehicles.

2. Traffic Cameras!—Here's a neat idea. Stop by the Cop Shop and get a tour of the dispatch area. You may find that there's banks and banks of traffic cameras up on the walls. If you're rolling big through even modestly controlled intersections, wave! You're on closed-circuit TV!

3. Citizens and Cellphones—If you're going for the full monty and that long coast-to-coast chase—be aware that with the abundance of communications available to motorists, they may call you in. Yeah, 911. "There's a very bad motorcyclist" calls aren't unheard of. Remember that "Report Drunk Driving by Calling #xxx on Your Cellphone"? "Report Aggressive Drivers by Calling #yyy on Your Cellphone" ain't far behind.

4. Interagency Cooperation—Yup, in the ten years since 9/11, the Feds have poured billions into updating and integrating your county and state dispatch systems. Big Bro very much wants one hand of law enforcement to know what the other is doing. Also, to save dough you'll find things like a

single dispatch center handling *all* EMS and all local, county, and state units in an area. In other words, running may poke a very big, very organized beehive.

All these things were different "in the day." Today, I wouldn't run simply because they'll use a "Pursuit Intervention Technique" on your bike. And the guys with the guns are rightfully much more nervous than they were back in the day. Oh, and the guy with the gun is always right. Do what they tell you. Failure to follow a lawful command is a crime and can lead to a, shall we say, electrifying experience.

I would also suggest you check state law. In Oregon, tap the ton (100 mph) and they give you the free impound and a ride to jail—that's the law now to my understanding. Several states and municipalities never really had hardcore fleeing statutes—now they've been beefed up. Running now could have the same effect on your bike as if it were stuffed with cocaine—they'll take it and sell it to pay your fees. Ask around in Florida.

A couple last thoughts: Even in the day, if you got pulled over and went all jailhouse-lawyer/high-school-civics on an officer they didn't like it. If you get pulled over, man up and shut up. Sign and slide away. Why? Because as you're lecturing Johnny Law about how in the Federalist Papers the founders were pretty clear that freedom of movement meant you don't *need* a driver's license, he might decide that, instead of laughing at that alligator clip you're using to hold on your plate, he's really looking at drug paraphernalia.

Yeah there are bad cops and really obnoxious cops, but most are just guys trying to help out and make a difference. The danger of pulling a runner or flashing big attitude is that the cops stop treating you like a descent guy—they start treating you like *you're* an ass.

Is it OK to pull a runner now because ole Captain Crash pulled a runner back in the day? I dunno—is it OK to rob banks because Jesse James got away with it? Should you bust out an illegal maneuver because I got away with it thirty years ago? Let me ask this: Have you ever heard of someone successfully defending themselves in court with "But *he* did it back in the day!"

Didn't think so. Don't blame others for your decisions— own it.

COMPLACENCY

Ever been to a train wreck? I have, several in fact—a couple of run-of-the-mill derails and a bunch of train/automobile collisions. Car versus train never ends well for the car. In fact, I don't think the train really knows it ever hit anything. There's just too dang much mass. By the time a few thousand tons of train smacks a ton of car, well, it is a wild scene. One shocking thing I learned was that when a train hits a car it actually accelerates the car sideways—that pushing it down the track half a mile business—and, as it accelerates, the thing with the most mass in the car accelerates the slowest. This means that the train will physically tear the car from around the motor. The body of the car is torn off the motor, and the motor rolls away by itself. At the third train versus car wreck I was at, I saw a pickup wrapped around the front of the train about half mile down the tracks from the crossing, and there was this big diesel engine sitting in the ditch next to the tracks. I asked a state trooper, "What's up with that?" and he explained it to me. Apparently violent engine removal isn't that uncommon.

At the time I was working as a news photographer for the local ABC affiliate. In a medium-sized market like Boise,

Idaho, you get to know the first responders. Folks never really think about this, but first responders tend to be open, friendly people. They may seem a little standoffish at the scene of an emergency, but that's because they're busy; they're doing their thing. Catch a fireman, policeman, or paramedic after the show's over and things slow down and they are pretty chatty. That's how I found out about extreme complacency.

Here's the deal: That train/truck wreck where the engine was torn out? Sitting at that crossing you have a solid mile of visibility each way down the tracks. Not to speak ill of the dead, but how do you *not* see that train coming? Trains have all these headlights, and one of them even rotates around— and about a quarter mile from a crossing they start blowing their horns! (Train secret: If you look as you're running parallel to a train track, you'll see a small white sign with a black X on it about quarter mile from an intersection with the tracks.)

Here's where I'm going: In talking to first responders they tell me (anecdotally) that most people who are involved with train/car collisions are close to home or at a crossing they use regularly. Likewise, they tell me that often the engineers report that the person driving the car or truck looked up at the train before proceeding into its path.

Sound familiar, my motorcycling friends? Familiar surrounding, eye contact, mash, boom, bang!

One of the interesting things that a trooper once said to me was this: "People see what they expect to see. They come up, haven't seen a train there for a long, long time, do not expect to see one, and then don't see the one that hits them. They see what they expect to see."

Ever wonder why there's that "Look Twice for Motorcyclists" campaign? Because we see what we expect to see. Most don't expect to see bikes, and so they don't look for them. People who aren't looking for things are complacent. Complacency is a false sense of security in a dangerous situation—like pulling up to a rail crossing and expecting not to see a train.

Complacency is a lot like carbon monoxide poisoning which, if you don't know the symptoms, you can ignore to your own demise. CO poisoning gives you a headache, makes you feel lethargic, dizzy, nauseous, and even (here's an old friend) impairs your judgment. You can be in the process of getting killed by carbon monoxide and convince yourself you must have eaten some bad clams, lay down for a nap, and never wake up. Hard to imagine? Trust me, if you heat your home with a woodstove you've started feeling funky and asked yourself, "Is it carbon monoxide or that three-day-old pizza I ate?" and gone to check the CO detectors to make sure they have batteries in them. Heating a home with a fire isn't a dangerous business. Take a little care, tend to the basics, and you'll be OK—but you have to be aware of the things that can go wrong. You see what you expect to see, and if you don't know the trouble, you won't look for it and you'll never see it.

Symptoms of complacency are as simple as this:

When was the last time you checked the air pressure in your tires? Did you check the tread that same time? Ever ridden a tire 'til the belts showed? How's that chain doing? Sprockets OK? Drive belt? Oil level? Ever change your plugs? What kind of brake life do you have left? What about brake fluid—ever change it? When was the last time you pulled the clutch in part way and checked for a frayed cable at the lever? Have you practiced an emergency stop in the last two weeks? Or a U-turn? Been caught off guard by a car or truck at an intersection? Had a "didn't see that coming—where'd it come from" moment? Or how 'bout a "WTF do I do now?" pucker?

A serious sign of a complacent rider is riding unaware, being surprised, or generally thinking more about next Sunday's game than the job at hand.

Why would riders just drift while riding? Because they have a decent skillset and have processing power to spare. Being good enough to let your mind drift is a pleasure and a pain. 100% attention to riding is a taxing thing, you have to work hard and focus your attention completely on riding. There comes a time when your skills are good enough that things just start happening. You're not thinking about downshifting; you're simply doing it. This could be the reason that after being trained, newbie riders have a lower crash rate for six months to a year; after that their crash rates match untrained riders. Could be that they become complacent.

Imagine what it would be like to be driving home, and as you're crossing those railroad tracks for the umpteenth time, suddenly, as the familiar thump of the first rail hits your steering axle, you look up and there's a train right on top of you. Be honest. You've had that moment on your bike before except it was a car that suddenly appeared in the lane into which you were merging. (And you blamed the car—don't worry I do that, too—even though it was on *us* not them.)

A complacent rider stops looking and just rides. I'll even offer that, after a couple years of crash-free riding, it's possible to forget the idea that you might crash. Your ego starts telling you that you're too smart to wreck. Sure, other "less skilled" riders might, but not you!

The minute you start thinking you've got something in the bag, figure on it biting you. As repetition of route or routine dulls your brain and autopilot guides you through your regular rides, you've become a wreck waiting to happen. You know when you're along for the ride, instead of controlling the ride. Take the hint, take charge, and don't become a victim of habit. You don't want to be the poor guy who looked at the train and didn't see it.

LIVE IN THE FUTURE

On your motorcycle you cannot afford to live in the past; you can live in the moment, but if you become caught in the moment then you risk spending your riding career responding to events around you instead of creating the moment you're in. Boy, howdy, that sounded all super philosophical...which it should...but shouldn't because we're talking some really practical advice here. Back in the day when I was taught to drive a semi tractor trailer my instructor was simply the full time driver the company had. His technique was pretty simple: watch me, then you do it. There was one thing he was adamant to the point of brutality about: if you're not driving a quarter mile ahead of yourself it's too late.

That simple concept has saved my bacon innumerable times. What's easily lost here is that an active interest in the future makes the present much more manageable because you have a reasonable expectation of what and why things are happening. What is a reasonable expectation? Let me show you.

I teach high school for a full-time living. The first day of class can be very telling; it's your first "eyes on" with new students. I am lucky because I will have about sixteen to twenty students who I will carry for three years. I start with approximately 100 to 120 in the first year class, and retention for the second year drops that number to about forty or fifty. By the time a student reaches his third year, to complete the program, I have twenty or so. Every year I get 100 or more new faces walking through my door. One of the things I have to do is make some quick reads; like the kid who's late to the first day of class has one of a couple of problems—either he can't manage his time well, he gets lost easy, or he doesn't put a premium on first impressions.

Here's another: If a kid comes through my door texting as he walks in, then I probably want to keep an eye on that child, because he is *texting as he walks in the door!* Isn't it clear? He is having a conversation as he comes in. What are the odds that I'm witnessing the end of that conversation? I'm gonna put a mental check next to that kid, and if he takes a sudden, intense interest in his own knees I'm gonna ask for the dang phone. Likewise, if a bundle of three kids come in playing slap and tickle and sit together, that means they're pals, and what do pals do? They play slap and tickle and disrupt my class. In this situation, I'll actually go over and tell them, "I don't use a seating chart unless I have to—do you understand what I'm saying to you?" Usually they understand and cooperate; if they don't, then I make a seating chart with three or four names on it, with those names in the individual corners of the room, and I tell the class that if your name's on the chart, sit in your seat; if it's not, sit where you want. The next step is offering not to use the chart next time if things are better that day. Oddly, my chatty students realize that by behaving themselves they can sit where they want. In other words, they start living in the future, planning the future, and making their future more pleasant.

I don't like to be surprised by student behavior. There are clear cues they send that tell me what they are probably going to do. Those cues allow me to have a strategic plan—a big plan for what I'm going to do. I learn that some students need to be called on, or they'll blurt answers out because they want to be noticed so badly. Others need me to wait until I've got a fat, juicy meatball going right down the middle so I can give it to them to hit. I can plan ahead and make things go much more easily and productively. Does that mean that students never surprise me? Trust me, when you're trying to get to the end of the Golden Age of Television (this really happened) and a kid holds up a hand-written sign on a piece of binder paper saying, "Mr. Allen HELP ME!" it can catch you out. Just like when you walk over and quietly ask, "What can I do for you?" and in a normal speaking voice she answers, "I'm pregnant, and I need to call my Mom to remind her to bring her paystub to the meeting at Health and Welfare today." Did not see that one coming; who could?

As a rider in traffic or even on a canyon run, you need to be living out in the future more. Predicting everything is impossible, but having a strategy and acting on it will get you out from behind the eight ball and back in control of your ride. We often hear the words *"I had to lay 'er down"* from riders. I believe that one of the things riders are saying with that comment is, "I got surprised—I just didn't see it coming and didn't know what to do when it did."

When you are riding your motorcycle, surprises are bad things. Oh sure, there are pleasant surprises like, "Look! A pie sale at the diner," and, "Thank goodness someone put a gas station right here," or, "Really, just a warning? Thanks officer!" But the hard reality of things is that if you are surprised it's usually because something you didn't expect to happen did. That is half of the "I didn't see it coming and didn't know what to do when it did" equation, which means you've rounded second base on your way to an accident. It's like a married man inside the strip club with his paycheck; things could very easily go strikingly, terribly, life-changingly, divorce attorney wrong. Wait—in that situation where's the surprise? A married guy in a bordello with cash—simply explaining being there is going to get you some road rash. The problem isn't being in the club with cash, the problem is being in the club at all. Standing outside the club you should have figured out this was a bad plan. Getting out of the car you should have seen it. Getting into the car with a load of just out of college news interns should have been a sign things were going, shall we say, askew? A little living in the future and you're not in the strip club with your paycheck ready for disaster to strike your marriage or relationship. Call me old school, if you wish, but I believe married men should have a space cushion around things like strip clubs—simply being seen in the proximity of one can lead to misunderstandings.

Yup, living a little farther in the future will help you out. If you ride the bike to a bar are you really surprised you had a beer? Was it an accident that to be the prince of beer, you got to know the king of beers? Come on, you rode a motorcycle to a bar, for hell's sake! I'm not saying don't go to the bar, but if you do it on a bike you're rounding second and headed for a statistical home run. However, knowing you are in danger is the first move to staying out of danger. Fine, go to the bar, but your vigilance level has to be through the roof—you have to remember that a third to a half of all motorcycle fatalities have a measurable blood alcohol count. Not drinking is an excellent strategic idea.

Living a few steps ahead on the bike is absolutely necessary. Imagine you're at a stoplight and want to turn right. You're in the right lane and there is a bicycle lane. You're fourth or fifth in a line of traffic, and none of the cars in front of you are signaling to make a right turn. Whatcha gonna do? First, you remember that old rule, "Never pass on the right." But, jeepers, there's soooo much room and nobody is signaling right. They're not even moved over at all. So, being nineteen, you decide to go for it because, well you're nineteen and the traffic is all stopped. With a dedicated twist of the throttle you pull out into the bike lane and start up to the intersection. Right about then the light goes green, and that tan Aries K moves hard right directly in front of you without signaling. Fortunately, you're riding a dual-sport so you simply jump the curb up onto the sidewalk and avoid the bus bench.

In the past I've always told that story as a "Stupid people don't signal...grrrr" story, but in reality I wound up driving on the sidewalk due to my own inability to fully read the situation. Yes, passing on the right is bad and you shouldn't do it, however, the thing that got me wasn't just *where* I was, but it was also *when* I was. Those cars had stood stationary for a good, long time before I decided to act. A smarter rider would have simply said, "The light is probably about to change. When these cars start moving one might be turning right and I'll get in a bind." If that first car doesn't move, then odds are the ones behind it are pinned in place, but once the light goes green and the cork is out, all bets are off. Living in the future is about accounting for variables, having a reasonable expectation of what's about to happen, and being ready to act if those reasonable things don't happen.

Live further in the future on your rides. Think about what's happening around you and why. What are the consequences? What are you going to do? Be *pro*-active not *re*-active.

And don't pass on the right. It's a bad thing.

Freeway Traffic

Ah, the super slab, the heart of the American highway system. Thank you President Eisenhower—no really, it is wonderful; coupled with the American rail system, it connects the country, intertwines our state economies, and you can get there from here. It's an engineering marvel. If you want to really see how wonderful it is try to get from Sacramento to Salt Lake City without using it. Good luck with that, let me know how that goes.

In the US, the width of a lane is dictated by the amount of truck traffic it carries. *Truck* traffic, not auto; the more trucks, the wider the lanes need to be. In realistic terms you're gonna find lanes between twelve and fifteen feet wide. On interstates, figure twelve. One of the key things to remember about interstates, freeways, expressways, or turnpikes is that as a general rule they are designed for interstate commerce, and that means trucks. The second thing they are designed to do is move as much humanity as quickly and efficiently as possible. If you can find me an traffic engineer who'll say, "Yeah, we take motorcycles into account when designing an eight lane highway to connect two moderately sized cities!" I'll buy you both dinner. To save myself buying too many dinners let me put this caveat in: Motorcycles are not primary users and as such are, at best, an afterthought in highway design.

You should remember that. Highways are not designed for motorcycles, so act accordingly.

Being on the highway is like being in the "Black Friday" crowd that is flowing through a store. You know, the day after Thanksgiving when zillions of people line up and rush the gate at five a.m. to get a screaming deal on a moderate laptop. I've been inside the store with a camera and documented that dash—the flow in the doors, the pushing, the flow as people run down main aisles, cut over to different lanes, merge back in after a detour to sporting goods, the works. That flow of motivated, focused, and self-centered shoppers is a lot like the interstate. It's a bit of a free for all.

Oh, people have manners out there, usually because of a fraternal bond. When I drove a truck, I pulled a flatbed forty-five footer or a set of twenty-seven/twenty-three foot doubles. Truckers are good to each other. They communicate, like flashing lights to let that guy passing you know he's clear, and then he blinks, "Thanks." As riders, we all wave at each other to try and say, "Hi, you're not alone." (The back side of The Wave is that giving it is reaching out for a contact and when you're in the soup, it's nice to have someone acknowledge you're there.)

A couple of tips for survival on multilane roads, especially large commercial and commuting pathways:

1.   Realize your size. You are the smallest, most vulnerable thing out there; you just are. I don't care how small the car, it's got a safety cage, airbags, fenders, and seatbelts. In the best case riders have a helmet, jacket, gloves, pants, and boots. If you're having difficulty feeling the vulnerability imagine this: You're riding in the back of a pickup truck in your gear— would you be comfortable jumping out into the number two lane at 65 mph? At 5 p.m. on a Friday?

2.   Act accordingly. If you're the smallest and most

vulnerable, you need to be the most alert and aware. Know who and what's around you. Know what lane you need to be in and when. If you simply roll out onto the freeway and figure everybody else is gonna take care of you, you're wrong, and you might be dead wrong.

3. Have a safety bubble—some call it a space cushion—call it what you want, but space is time and time gives you a chance to make wise decisions. So have some extra space around you. Don't ride in other folks' blind spots if you can possibly avoid it. Do give yourself some following distance—a car or SUV can easily straddle things that can make your life miserable or even knock you on your butt. What sorts of things? Ladders, hammers, and skillsaws! Car batteries. Dead animals. Paint cans. Lawn chairs and teddy bears. Some stuff you can surmount, some you can't. Potholes and surface imperfections will pass easily under a car and leave you with the Snake River Canyon to jump. By keeping your distance it is simply easier to see it and then avoid it, rather than have an emergency swerve, surmount, or jump. Give yourself space and you give yourself time.

4. Find a lane you're comfortable in. I am *not* comfortable in the outside lanes. I prefer the fast lane. Why? Because no one is busting through it to get on or off the freeway. Let's face it, the far right lane is busy and full of people accelerating and merging and decelerating and exiting; sometimes both at once...from either side. I find the fast lane generally affords some emergency run off to the left, and people are not cutting across my bow to get to the restroom at the gas station. The downside is that the fast lane *is* the fast lane and you need to be willing to flow with traffic. Getting into the fast lane and...ahhh...demonstrating the proper freeway speed can annoy other users and actually turn you into a target. I am not telling you to speed. I am simply letting you know that the fast lane is full of aggressive, hustling people; getting out there and holding them up can be dangerous to your own health. If the lane is moving faster

than the speed limit and you're not comfortable going like a bunny, get out; find a better place to ride. Don't get sucked in over your head. This is a good place for me to say that if you don't like riding on the freeway, *don't*. Find another route. It's OK. Better to be late than maimed.

5.   Look for clues. Once drivers start considering moving around, they often look around; drivers constantly looking up at their rearview and flipping glances off to the right are probably looking to move to the right. This is a majority behavior. Most people look before they leap, that doesn't mean they *see*. Don't assume they see you, even when they're looking directly at you. Have an escape plan, whether it's swerving, braking, or accelerating.

6.   Share your clues. Signal. You can use both the electronic kind and the hand kind; it makes you more visible and clearly states your intentions. Turn your head and look, don't just glance; get a look and get the info you need. Oh, honking is a clue too. How better to say, "Here I am!" than a quick beep on the horn? As much as riders don't like to be surprised, we should not be surprising other users. It's a hypocrisy issue; we can't afford to be the folks complaining about crappy drivers and then run around being crappy riders.

Apex and the Line

There are a lot of different ways to swing the bat at the idea of "the Apex" and "the Line." I would like to start with a little disambiguation: apexes and line selection are not just for racing and racers. Yes, racers worry about the line and where they put their apexes; they do this to pick up fast lap times and to avoid crashing. That last one, avoiding crashing—being able to negotiate a turn successfully—is where crossover to street skills comes into play. As recently as 2009, about fifty percent of riders killed were in single-vehicle accidents, generally meaning they "ran wide in a turn" then "struck a fixed object" or were "thrown from the motorcycle." Knowing what an apex is and how to select a proper line will help keep you on the road and on your bike. Could this knowledge potentially increase the speed at which you ride? Absolutely yes, but in this situation we're talking a skill that street and race hold in common, and like a gun, can be used for good or for evil. Motorcycling is about personal responsibility, making your own choices, and living your own life; you can use what is discussed for your own benefit or to your own detriment.

The apex is the point in a turn when you are closest to

the inside of the curve. Think of it this way: You're in a left hand turn and there's a double yellow line. As you make that turn you have two basic choices: try and match that curve perfectly (an acceptable course) or to open or relax that curve using the "outside, inside, outside" line. In a left hand turn, if you enter the turn from the right third of the lane, move to the center of the lane at the center of the turn, and finally exit the turn in the right third of the lane you've just made a classic "outside, inside, outside" turn with a "center apex." Run it in your mind a moment and you'll see the curve you actually *chose* to ride was more relaxed and open than the curve of the road.

I know that there are people out in the world who say, "You never need to worry about apexing; that swoopy-doopy stuff is for racing. Just get in one wheel track or the other and follow the road." They are, as I mentioned before, right; however, it is vital to understand that when you're riding one of the things you want to have is options. By simply picking a track and following it and ignoring the idea of picking a line, you've cut your options off and potentially locked yourself onto a path without seriously thinking about why you're there. The average lane is somewhere between ten and twelve feet wide and may even have run out over the fog line. Why on earth would you want to pick an eighteen inch wide swath and say, "That's mine!" and struggle to stay there? We owe it to ourselves to control our path of travel and to create situations where we don't end up saying, "I don't know what happened. I tried but the bike just couldn't make the turn." That is the excuse of someone who went into a turn without a plan and came out an insurance claim.

The phrase "think outside the box" isn't new. It suggests going outside the conventional norms to find an answer. One thing I never hear anyone say is, "Expand your box." If you're a fan of riding the wheel rut, you need not get out of the box. Simply expand your box. Look at all the possibilities you are giving up, the options you are ignoring. Let's talk about the apex tool I keep in my box. I like using late apexes on my rides up in the mountains or in the country, and I don't do it to pick up speed. I do it to increase my field of vision. By holding an outside line until I can see the exit of a turn it allows me more visual lead, and I can see other users earlier and make better decisions on when I want to tighten the line and head for the exit. I will also see imperfections in the road surface, objects on the road, and the exit sooner—not much, mind you, but every little second helps. There is another advantage in left-handers, by keeping to the outside at the entrance of a left I avoid other users who are running wide on their exit—I'm keeping the most space cushion I can, and if that logging truck is running a little wide where would *you* rather be? Mentally locked into the left third of the lane or on the outside looking in?

The idea of the line is to open up the turn, which, yes, can mean you open the throttle up a little as well. That's why racers look for the perfect line. Racers are also on a track, with instruction, corner workers, first aid, and emergency services nearby, which is why they can hang it all out and hunt the perfect line through that turn. Racers can worry about mid-corner speed and exit speed and maximizing it. Street riders, on the other hand, are not looking for fast times. Street riders are looking for the most information possible, the safest path of travel, and (I'll admit) a little fun. Coming into a turn way too hot isn't fun, not being sure you can safely negotiate a turn you're already in isn't fun, being scared on a bike isn't fun, and getting hurt on a bike sucks the big one. One of the things that consciously thinking about your line does for you is it helps you pick an appropriate entry speed. It's simply the act of looking ahead, realizing things appear a little tight up there, and slowing down. If you fall into the trap of riding the wheel ruts, you're in a place where you're not looking ahead and planning—you're watching and following the wheel ruts.

Ever been to a party? I have. Ever been to a party with lots of intoxicated nineteen and twenty-year-olds? I have too. I remember one such party. I went into the kitchen and there were angels and devils in there because it was a Halloween party. The angels and devils were trying to make strawberry daiquiris without much success. Being the helpful sort, I watched the mayhem for a few moments before asking if assistance was needed. The deal was the blender didn't work and the angels and devils were sorely vexed because they had put in the strawberries, the ice, and the booze and they couldn't get a daiquiri to happen. They had all the right things but were suffering from one small problem—a problem I had spied but was not going to point out right away—the blender was unplugged. Inebriated people are fun because they are impaired, so they have poor judgment and poor observational skills. I decided I wanted a daiquiri, too, and began to plead and cajole asking for one. It was giggletastic.

Eventually, as a little devil was getting ready to pour me a ice cube daiquiri, I stopped and said, "Can I offer some advice?" To which I got blank stares. "Plug the blender in," says I. Laughter, red faces, the whirr and grind of ice being pulverized...drinks for all (and an appreciative and cute girl in a devil costume isn't a bad thing either). What's important here is that when you're on the road you have a full ten to twelve feet to work with—it's like the blender sitting there full of daiquiri mix, ice, and booze. You should know how to use it. However, if you decide to simply follow the wheel ruts it's like having a ready blender but not plugging it in. Choosing a line gives you power to fully utilize the road in front of you.

Using an active planning strategy has its own risks as well. You can get suckered into the racing mind set and end up in a place where you're not looking for space and vision, but rather trying to increase your entry and exit speeds. Simply put you risk getting into a race with yourself. Remember, you're still on a ten foot wide strip of road; most racetracks are thirty feet or more wide. Your path of travel should keep you away from other users and not put you in danger of colliding with them.

Another danger that planning a racing type line presents is that you might be tempted to put that front tire right on that yellow line—to use every bit of that glorious lane. This means you're putting yourself right up against the edge of the other users' space. Potentially, even riding with your bike in your lane, your noggin might be sticking out into the other lane and could connect with oncoming traffic. If you're crowding the center line for speed, what happens when someone doing the same thing comes the other way?

Plugging in the blender makes for better drinks. It also means you can drink too much. Know what an apex is; use the outside/inside/outside technique to open up corners; but most importantly, use lane position to increase your vision, visibility, and space cushion.

Left Foot Down at Stops
and Trail Braking

Ever see two chipmunks fight? Over a peanut or a quarter of a hot dog bun? Them little suckers can absolutely go to town in little mixed martial chipmunk arts death matches. Sounds stupid, but if you've seen it you know what I mean— all for half a peanut; or if you play your cards right it's for an empty peanut shell. Metaphorically speaking, I've seen this fight in online motorcycle forums as well.

It's about which foot to put down when you come to a stop. Really. Go Google it. You'll be surprised by the vehemence of the arguments. The orthodox position is that you keep your right foot on the peg, downshifting with the left until you're in first, then you put your left foot to the ground and the right can hold the bike with the rear brake. Let me warn you—post that you put the right down first or both down at once and you'd think it was a crime against humanity—like you'd just admitted going to the town next door and doing a little ethnic cleansing. Not everybody seems to care, but some folks, they get pretty revved up, and it becomes a regular chipmunk knife fight.

For my two bits: I downshift with the left, and when I'm all done downshifting, I put left to the ground first. Then, I often (horrified valley girl "OMG" gasp) put down my right as well. Yes, the shame is nearly unbearable, but I often sit at stoplights with both feet down. Why? 'Cause I'm old and it don't hurt to stretch my legs. Also, I may have the lovely Mrs. Crash on back, and it gives me decidedly more stability to have both feet down. Oddly, some folks find that right foot down to be a shocking bit of sloth, which is OK by me, because I really don't care much about what you think of my comfort; I'm more worried about me.

The left foot down first argument is always interesting to me because it's another one of those areas where riders piss and shake their fists about *how* instead of thinking about *why?* Yeah...why would you want to go left down first? Could be control...could be the crown of the road makes for a shorter reach and you're not tipping out...could be you've got a blown right knee and can't support your weight well with it.

Wait. Did I just say you might go left down first because you've got a bad right knee? But, wait, wha...what if you've got a bad *left* knee? Do you just suck it up and tough it out? *Of course not.* If you've got a hitch in yer get-a-long, and you're better at supporting that bike with your right leg, go ahead and put it down first. Why? Yes, *why* is important—you do it because it gives you better control of your motorcycle at a standstill. Don't be a nit if you physically are better off putting your right down.

I can hear the mumbling. Can you hear the mumbling? Someone's pissed that I just said, "It's OK to put your right foot down first." The accent sounds "thumb of Michigan"... Someone's upset that I broke an absolute and added a subjective assessment. Bummer.

This is a lot like braking in a turn. Which you can do, if you're careful, just don't tell anyone I told you that. See, in a quest to reach the lowest common denominator, we kind of get into this place in motorcycling where we give a rule, and even though it's not really an absolute rule, it's perceived as an absolute. I was teaching a beginner class the other day and sure enough the words were coming out of my mouth, "Complete all braking before the turn," and, "When do we finish braking? That's right before the turn," and, "What don't we want to do in a turn? That's right—Braking." All of which is completely accurate and absolute rubbish at the same time. You can brake in a turn, the technique is called "trail braking" and it's an advanced technique, so with beginners we don't want to get into it...because, really, who wants a rank beginner to be trail braking to the apex of a corner in a basic riding class? The solution is not to talk about it, which leads to the belief that you can't brake in a turn. Which, at times, leads to wonderfully confused riders who start asking questions like, "Why did those safety guys lie to me?" We didn't. We nuanced the word braking to mean before the turn...but you can brake in a turn. It's called trail braking. Don't hate me. By the by, trail braking is really an excellent racing technique that used to go something along the lines of "brake until you see Jesus standing there at the apex waving at you to gas it and go."

Getting all your braking done before the curve is better for less spirited riding.

See the conundrum? If you tell the truth, you have a half hour of explaining to do. Then if an inexperienced rider grabs an advanced technique and tries and dies? Oooooh... wait...I told them to do what? If you're teaching "how" then you actually make teaching easier (never brake in a turn), but only until the student gets conflicting information—then the student can get confused. It turns out, some folks like to be told exactly what to do and then stick to it like Superglue.

Another "foot down" example; when teaching riders to stop, the language can go:

1. Roll off throttle.
2. Pull in clutch.
3. Apply both brakes.

4. Downshift.
5. Stop.
6. Left foot to the ground.

Now, that doesn't seem toooo difficult does it? Until you look at steps five and six—that's where some folks really suffer. See, I read that to say, "As the bike stops, left foot to ground." Oddly, some folks read this as "motorcycle stops, then you balance, then you put your left foot down." Doesn't seem like that big of a deal, does it? We're not talking about parsing words in a major league contract—we're talking about stopping and putting your left foot down, or are we talking about stopping while putting your left foot down? It is different, ain't it?

At this point in the conversation, *why* actually becomes important. You do want to be careful when you put your foot down, because if you are trying to paddle to a stop or trying to stop a moving motorcycle with your feet, you are risking serious injury. In the process of stopping you need to get your foot down in a manner that doesn't place your ability to Cha-Cha and Macarena at serious risk. Professionals wrestle with how to impart good skills and habits to beginners. Part of that struggle is how to communicate those skills and habits to newbies. The problem is that some people take words and make them mean things that aren't intended. That risk is high enough that folks who write curriculum struggle with word selection or simple word order. Is it "stop and put your foot down" or "as you stop, put your foot down"? Now, suddenly those seem very different, don't they?

With that in mind, think about teaching curves, brakes, and throttle and all the bad things that can happen if you get on the binders in a turn; sprinkle in a new rider who parses every word you say, and come up with a way to teach braking to beginners.

I'd dump trail braking, too, and drive home a rule to live by that is sound and reasoned like, "complete your braking before the turn." What happens next is that excellent advice gets taken to heart and then becomes carved in stone. Yes, it's carved in stone—and it absolutely works—but if you grab it and lock onto it as the only truth—if you don't see that it's a good rule, but there are situations where it bends and flexes and has particle and wave qualities—you're hurting yourself. Keep some flexibility in your thinking. Think more about *why* when you're looking at *how*. Getting stuck on absolute orthodoxy to word order, without knowing the *why* behind that word order, is intellectually lazy, and a mentally lazy rider is a rider at risk.

Be curious. Be interested. Be open to the possibilities that a "foundational" rule is one you build on. Be open to the possibilities.

THE WAVE

OK, this is my take on "The Wave." I bring nothing special to this; I have not done exhaustive research, or any at all for that matter. I wasn't there when the first wave was thrown. The Wave is just a thing that has always seemed to be around. Somewhere back in the haze of time, I imagine that some pre-Columbian American was riding his sloth through the rainforest and seeing another rider out on his sloth simply threw down the first wave. The sloth and pre-Columbian are there because, again, in my nonexistent research this seems to be an American oddity; Europeans do not appear to be plagued by The Wave and how to react to it. Why did the first sloth/llama/crocodile riders wave to each other? I believe it goes to fraternity. I found myself first waving to people when I was four-wheeling. Out in the middle of nowhere you would be coming down a trail and see another truck or jeep and as you pass—what do you do? It's awkward! You don't want to look stuck up, and you're forty miles in the middle of nothing, and that guy might end up being the guy you have to flag down for help, so you give a charitable, friendly wave.

You just said, "Hey, I'm one of us. Have a good day. Help me later if I need it?" It's a way of not being alone when you're alone. Nowadays on a bike there's all these waving etiquette problems like:

Do I wave at other brands?

Do I wave at other styles?

Do I wave if the passenger does, but the driver does not? (I don't want to look like I'm hitting on anyone.)

What if I wave, and they don't?

What if they wave, and I don't?

Do I do the two-fingered thing or all five?

Can I just raise my fingers off the grip—is that enough?

See what I mean? I've only been riding thirty years and still haven't figured it out. Back in the day, there was a little of it going on but recently it's a wave-o-rama out there. People are pissed because you wave; people are pissed if you don't. What the frickity frack is going on out there? With the Earth, Air, Fire, and Water motif in mind, here are my thoughts on The Wave in four parts.

The Wave Part 1 (Earth)

In some motorcycle shop somewhere, there stands a man or woman looking at a motorcycle, and he or she is thinking about all the things he or she can do with that motorcycle. Standing there is the flower of a childhood dream, or the reaching out for that midlife crisis, or simply an idea that took root and grew. No matter what, there are a lot of thoughts going through people's heads. I believe that some of those folks are looking forward to waving at other riders. Connecting, or wanting to be part of something, is pretty darn normal; people want to associate themselves with larger things and groups. Just think about all those jerseys and caps and bumper stickers and beer koozies with a team or company logo. Come on, you've got some kind of T-shirt or trinket with a brand logo on it—motorcycle brand, or tire, or pistol...

Simply walking down the street with that logo on is a

way to set ourselves apart from the masses and still be part of something, something smaller and more manageable, something we can get our minds around. It's like we want to be part of something more than ourselves, but less than all of us together.

Our rider, or even the wannabe rider, is looking for that fraternity that comes not from knowing someone, yet still being able to look at a stranger and say, "We are brothers." Think about how your heart jumps a half a beat when you see someone wearing a T-shirt from that obscure band you used to listen to in high school. The moment of familiarity, of seeing someone who validates those CDs you ordered from London, is important because that other person is secretly reaching out to you. To the uninitiated, riders are part of a brotherhood, and The Wave is our not-so-secret sign, and new riders long for the camaraderie of being able to wave—and that's OK by me.

The Wave Part 2 (Air)

The newbie wave might not be OK by me. You know that guy—you've ridden with him—he waves at everything on two wheels—bicycles, scooters, cars up on blocks with only two rims left on, every freaking thing. Now that's OK, I understand that once you learn the not-so-secret handshake you need to bust it out and rock it a little. I like it when puppies wag their tails, and for a new rider waving can be like wagging his tail. Unfortunately for the rest of us, it can become like peeing on the couch. Yes, puppies are supposed to pee on things, but eventually they need to be house broken. I'm not saying don't wave. I'm saying you don't need to wave at a rider who's eight lanes away going the other direction.

I believe that some of those wavers (Is that a word?) are doing it because they believe they are supposed to. That is OK by me. Do what you got to do. Eventually all that waving, all those low down two-finger salutes don't hurt a dang thing. I've looked in the mirror at a rider going away and realized, "Oops he waved, and I didn't." If that was you then you have my apologies. It wasn't an intentional slight. I was just not paying attention. If you dig waving—if it's your thing and you can't get enough—then to twist Al Davis's words, "Just wave, baby, wave."

If it buoys your soul and melts your butter, wave, baby, wave.

The Wave Part 3 (Fire)

Everyone (yes, every single stinking one of us—even those of you who are gonna say, "Not me!"), every one of us, gets sick of The Wave once in a while. You wax and wane. Sometimes you wave, sometimes you don't; sometimes you wave back, sometimes you give the mental finger. I admit my evil—I will on occasion do a "get even" wave. The "get even" wave is that wave you throw while in a turn. Yeah, you take your hand off the bars in a turn (tighter the better) and mentally you say, "Chew on that!" I don't do that often; it's pretty rare in fact; but it's just one of those things that when you've been waving your brains out for twenty or thirty bikes and you get tired of it, you just do it. Yes, it is cruel. I've seen the poor bastard going the other way waggle their bike as they try to decide if they should try and throw it back—which leads me to a real problem: control of your motorcycle.

Waving requires you to take a hand off the bars. Yes, it's your clutch hand. (How important is that, really?) You let go of the bars and then grab them back again, and for some riders that is an unsettling idea. If you're a hardcore safety fan, you may want to jump ahead a paragraph. Occasionally, I will take both hands off the bars. There, I said it and I feel better. Once in while on a straight road, I take my hands off the bars, and just like I did when I was ten years old on a Stingray bicycle, I let the bike steer itself. Now, if you threw up in your mouth a little bit, that's OK—I am not suggesting we all go riding around no-handed—I am suggesting that motorcycles like to go in a straight line, and I am admitting that I like to let them do that once in a while. With that in mind, think about the newbies or the riders with limited experience who have to take their hands off the controls to wave at you. Imagine what they must feel like when they are watching you coming, heading into a turn, trying to figure out whether to wave or not. Will he? Should I? I'm countersteering! Can I just lift two fingers? Yikes.

The Wave Part 4 (Water)

A new rider lost in the complexity of simply operating the motorcycle might not wave at you. A rider focused on the road in front of him may simply catalog you as "motorcycle— in his own lane, not a threat" and never see your wave. When I wax on about the "elements," I am always stuck by the tranquility of water and how all things can come to balance.

If you wave at me, I'll try to wave back if I see it and if I can. Often, I just realize, "Oh, they're waving," and all I can bust out is a head nod. There's no malice in not waving; I'm simply occupied with other things. If I wave and you don't, I don't mind. You've got things to do, places to be, and people to see; you may be preoccupied or simply uncomfortable letting go of the controls.

When I read online forums, I find all kinds of blather about "The Wave." There's pontification about who does and who doesn't and why they do or don't. There's acrimony in the words, and some angry people use The Wave as a means to drive yet another wedge into the motorcycle nation. Is the most important thing that happens on your ride whether or not some guy on a different brand waves at you? Does not getting a return wave really diminish who you are as a person? In a world where motorcycling is still trying to find its place at the transportation roundtable, is The Wave the thing we should be that worried about? I've heard it, you've heard it: "I hate those (insert brand or style here) guys. They never wave..." or "I hate those (insert brand or style here) guys, always waving at me..." The key word and the real problem is the word *hate*. I love motorcycles and motorcyclists. I love them all. We are all part and parcel of the best transportation device ever designed. Remember, bikes are the bacon of the transportation world; they are just flat fun, so why get wrapped up in finding things to hate about each other?

Me? I'll wave if I can—and if I can't, be generous and figure that I'm having so much freaking fun I forgot to.

LOUD PIPES

When it comes to loud pipes I am not a hater; in fact I have a loud bike, a pretty dang loud one. It's a 400cc single-cylinder supermoto with a full exhaust system on it. It's had the airbox cut to let more air in, and the carb has been jetted to make sure enough fuel pours into the system when it's wide open and hungry. Oh, and it makes a beautiful noise. Thump, thump, thump at idle and a heck of a roar when it's spun up. Why did I pull that EPA/DOT federally certified exhaust off and replace it with something else? I have two reasons. First, it goes faster now. Duh. It is tuned better, has more stonk, wheelies more easily, and has a more well-rounded throttle response. Second, it sounds cool as hell. When it idles it sounds like a helicopter, and when you whack it wide open it sounds—well—it sounds like it should sound: muscular, stout, and throaty.

Loud pipes are out there; people change their exhausts probably more than any other single thing. Just look on the web at the wide galaxy of aftermarket systems that are available. There are lots of people making aftermarket pipes for motorcycles, and it is all illegal. Yeah, go check those pipes you just put on the bike last year: Race only? Not for Street use? Doesn't meet EPA standards? Welcome to the club. There are very few aftermarket pipes that meet EPA noise standards. I know. Every single one I've bought comes with the same disclaimer: "Doesn't meet federal standards." Why do I buy them? Because on some bikes (especially single-cylinder ones) I think stock pipes underperform, and more to the point, they sound like poo...in a blender...that runs too slow. In Crash World some bikes need to sound right and that means a bit of an edge, a bit of a growl, maybe even a bit of a bite.

Even in Crash World there can be too much of a good thing, and a point where with a street bike you cross a line. I expect to have my ears bleed at the dragstrip; I would be disappointed if they didn't. On the street, in the QuickTrip parking lot, I don't expect to physically hurt when someone starts his bike. What really drives me nuts is the weak-sauce excuses you hear for those inanely loud pipes. Let me put this straight to you: Loud pipes don't save lives; they're pointed the wrong way to warn anyone you're coming, and the poor knucklehead behind you knows you're there, trust me. I find the "loud pipes save lives" argument akin to reading *Playboy* magazine because you really like the way it's bound. Yeah, I know, there's pretty girls who can't afford clothes in there, too, but you read it because the quality of the binding process is so very high.

BS. You read *Playboy* to see pretty girls without their clothes on, and you have a loud bike because it sounds cool. There. It's out. Loud bikes sound cool. So why demean yourself with a pandering argument about safety, when you could just own the fact you like a loud bike? There no shame in liking to make a sweet racket with your bike, so why hide it like it's something dirty? You're not a criminal pervert or a creeper; you just like a loud bike. It's not like you're admitting to being a pedophile. If you like the roar and thunder, or the rip and tear of a good pipe that is absolutely cool with me.

There is a "heads up" point we all need to have; there's

a point where our loud bikes start annoying other, less-enlightened people, and we need to know where that line is. Often, on my single-cylinder bikes, I would put on an exhaust with adjustable baffles. This means that I could run ten to twelve disks in the exhaust (sedate and good for sneaking out) or up to twenty-three (very loud; kill the engine a half mile from home and coast in). Having adjustable baffles allowed me to tune the bike to the situation. If I was going to go crazy, wanted big airflow and wanted big sound, I put in lots of disks, running the pipe wide open. If I wanted to tone it down and impress that new girl from So Cal's family, I took a bunch out and rolled up in stealth mode. (Oddly, her Dad wanted to know what it sounds like opened up—Way to go, Sir!)

Loads of exhausts today can be bought with an optional removable baffle. Put it in, quiet things down; take it out, spice it up. The ability to tune your exhaust can really be a nice feature, especially if you know that there are times and places you might want to tone it down. California recently took legislative action to curb loud pipes. It takes effect in a couple of years, and you won't be able to license a bike that has pipes that are beyond EPA standard. How does that happen? Loud pipes don't save lives; loud pipes annoy non-riders. Annoyed non-riders get into groups and start calling their state representatives and pretty soon some astute politically-minded state senator decides to appease the angry soccer moms and what's the easiest group to pick on? The one that's most fractured, like riders. Presto—suddenly bikes manufactured after 2013, in California need to have EPA stamped pipes... or pony up the dough when you get a ticket. Legislators get to say, "Look at what we did to end noise pollution," angry citizens get appeased, and cruiser riders blame sportbikers who blame cruiser riders, and now modding that new 2013 ride can be a little risky.

I, on the other hand, am a sick man: I like the idea of getting a fine for having a loud bike because people who have loud pipes should be emotionally invested and "all in."

Not only should you pay for the pipe, but you should be willing to say, "Yes, that's worth a $100 fine to me." Clearly I've hit my head too many times, but I think that kind of responsibility is admirable. Being able to say, "Yes officer, those are aftermarket pipes and the EPA does not approve. I'll happily sign on the line because, well, I love loud pipes and I'm ready to pay," brings with it some of that old school cowboy machismo that is missing when you run around whining about loud pipes being some kind of twisted safety gizmo. Like it loud? Own it. Eventually it might cost you cash, but you'll have my respect.

Own it. No excuses.

BIRD STRIKES

This is about bird strikes, not bird strike but bird strike*s*. Why the plural? Because this morning while on my way to teach a session of motorcycle training, I hit my second bird. The first bird strike I had was up on a mountain road, running at, shall we say, extra-legal speeds. Zipping along on a GSXR1100 (monster sportbike) next to a Forest Service heli-attack base and a small airport with ponderosa pines on one side and a runway on the other, I had a small bird hit me in the right shoulder/upper arm. It was a pretty good whack, but didn't cause a steering input or a change of course. For a split second I was aware of the bird and got just a mental flash of a picture before it entered the airflow around the bike and smacked me. Not to be graphic, but I believe I felt every bone in that bird break as it hit me.

Bird strikes are bad news for airplanes and engines as we all know from the "Miracle on the Hudson." A bird into a jet engine is a bit like dropping a fork into a blender—it's bad for the fork and bad for the blender. In my experience as a rider, a bird strike is...well...extremely awkward, but not life-threatening.

Before you get all bird-nervous and start searching the sky for kamikaze fowl let me whip this out and lay it on you: The reason I'm writing about bird strikes is that I've known a couple of riders who've smacked a bird once; but in my experience I'm the only person I know who's killed two birds while riding a motorcycle. What strange confluence of physics and luck culminates in poor Crash smacking into birds? I don't know. Frankly, I think that I hit birds, not the reverse; meaning I'm the thing carrying real speed; I'm the thing that when something crosses its path cleans it out like a freight train.

This morning during my second bird strike, I actually thought for a moment that it was a bat strike. With the sun only up for a few moments, I was traveling on my Honda Shadow Phantom at about 50 mph in a 50 zone; which means that I hit birds at legal *and* extra-legal speeds. There was a blur in my peripheral vision that was grey and black and then WHACK! Dead center of my chest gets thumped. It felt like when you get drilled with a fair sized water balloon. I believe it was a starling or it could have been a quail, but all I am sure of it was a lot of grey and black so I'm leaning starling, maybe six or eight ounces.

Should I mention that it stuck there a moment, and I shrugged/swatted/convulsed it off? Yes, it was gross and all old school heebie jeebies. I am not a young man. I've seen some gross stuff—been in the emergency room with a nephew because it was too rough for Mom or Dad to watch and someone needed to be there to talk a kid down. (Horse bite... on the cheek...150 odd stitches) I have had those moments in the exam room where you hold the finger up to the doc and say, "How do we fix *this?*" (Toothpick sized sliver embedded under the nail into the nail bed.) Out in the desert with my ranching in-laws I've seen some seriously grotesque veterinary field surgery. (Want to know what happens when a cow can't fully deliver a calf and it's half born and been dead a few days? No you don't! Nobody does.)

But a dead bird wedged by the wind on my chest? Icky! (Go ahead, wring your hands...I am.)

Here's my take on bird strikes: They happen and they may happen more often than I realize, but they are pretty dang rare. Should you spend your day being nervous about taking a bird strike? Nope. Are bird strikes a serious danger? Not that I can tell. A quick bit of research shows that there's no real stats on motorcycle bird strikes. It happens rarely. I would offer that hitting a larger bird like a turkey or pheasant could potentially be catastrophic due to the chances that as the bird's mass increases you're gonna get a bigger impact. However, in the real world you need to deal with a bird strike like you would any other unexpected violence to you or your bike: don't freak. Yep, remember that a suddenly violent steering input or braking input can put you on your butt; best to keep riding.

Let me touch on one other issue: The rabbit hole. Alice fell down the rabbit hole and the further she went, the weirder it got. Bird strikes are in the rabbit hole. You might hit a bird. Keep your wits and you'll be OK. If, as you read this, you're saying, "But I heard about a guy who hit a thrity-six pound turkey, and it got caught in his mesh jacket, and then clawed his eyes out and gave him cancer!" Fine. That's OK. Call somebody and get on a talk show. A common mistake for riders is questing for all the "but, what if" scenarios. That's what I call going down the rabbit hole—it's a waste of time and does nothing to protect you as a rider. Generally, it's people showing a basic fear or trying to look smart. Let's take a little trip down the bird strike rabbit hole, and then I'll throw the rope in to fish you out.

"What if I hit a bird in a turn?"

"What if I hit a bird in a turn with the sun in my eyes?"

"What if I hit a bird in a turn with the sun in my eyes, and I have brittle bone syndrome?"

"What if I hit a bird in a turn with the sun in my eyes, and

I have brittle bone syndrome, and there's a fully loaded fuel truck coming the other way, and it turns out I'm allergic to the bird and anaphylactic shock sets in, but I'm in a part of the country where they can't understand my accent, my tongue is swelling, and I'm not wearing clean underwear, but my left boot is smaller than my right, and there's debris on the road, and it's raining?"

Feel that suction pulling you down? Here's the rope: Don't freak out, no sudden inputs, no violent throttle changes; just keep riding. Yup, just keep riding—you hit a bird, it might hurt, but that doesn't mean the time has come to go all hizzy and pitch your bike down the road. A cool head and a steady hand will save your bacon from the unexpected. No matter how weird that thing is that happens to you keep your wits and keep on riding.

If something unexpected happens to me I shrug it off and keep riding.

A note: I live in a rural area with a tremendous amount of agriculture. I was out riding again early in the morning and noticed a shocking number of birds on and around the road. Turns out that the harvest has started—I'm not sure if it's barley, wheat, or something else, but trucks are spilling grain on the road. At intersections you'll find small piles of grain where it leaked out of overloaded or older trucks. That grain is also spread down the road by moving trucks. A thing to remember in farming areas would be that during the harvest, hungry (not angry) birds are on and around the road scavenging that grain. They are pretty dang bold about staring down cars. I assume it's a survival thing. As they struggle to get as much chow as possible, they'll wait to the last second to bail. Looking back, I believe my second bird strike was a starling scavenging on the side of the road that tried to fly back across the road and got drilled by me.

The harvest is a time of bounty for farmers, we should expect tractors and watch out for slow moving loads. We need to remember that our fine feathered friends are taking advantage of the situation as well. If you see birds on the road scavenging don't be afraid to honk the horn and scatter them before you get to them. Otherwise you might end up wearing one.

TAILGATERING

Well, slap a top hat on me and call me Daniel Webster, I just made up a word: "Tailgatering." It was easy and fun, required little craft, and totally screwed with the spell check function—all good things in Crash World. Speaking of screwing with things, when someone is actively engaging in tailgating you, the natural reaction is to screw with them. A serious brake check comes to mind...or there's that old toss a three-quarter inch nut over your shoulder trick...can't turn on the windshield wipers and pump a gallon of washer fluid out though...so, what to do with a tailgater?

Go Tailgatering! Yes, yes, I made the name up, and I admit tailgating is a deadly serious business. The idea is that if you are being tailgated then you need keep a cool head (relax), have a vigilant attitude (be aware of things all around you), and don't let the guy behind you dictate your behavior—stay in control of yourself. And now, the rules of Tailgatering.

1. Only you get to play. If the person behind you realizes you're playing he may attempt to join in, and frankly, he doesn't know how to drive well enough to be part of your party. If he knew how to drive he wouldn't tailgate, *ipso facto*,

they couldn't be part of the game anyway. The only intelligent operator during a game of Tailgatering is you.

2.   Never antagonize your playmate. Odds are he's asleep at the switch and simply following at his "normal" distance and is comfortable sitting back there at one or one-half second. If he feels you're dicking with him he might become hostile or aggressive, then no matter how long he spends in jail, you will be the one in rehab. Please remember that the operator of a car is at very little risk during a collision with a bike—accidental or intentional. Part of the goal of Tailgatering is to try and bend things back to a "safe" situation.

3.   Know when to quit. Yeah, you may need to make that lane change, or that exit, or turn off the main drag. To be simple, if it's a bad situation feel free to flee. If a tailgater has turned to a road rager then elude, evade, and park it up in a safe place. You probably have superior acceleration, braking, and turning. Most importantly your bike will slip between things a pursuing nutball can't. Simply going into a parking lot and slipping between parked cars can offer refuge and escape so you can get stopped and call for help.

With those basics under your belt lets discuss how to move your pieces on the board. Goal number one: increase your space cushion to the front. This is not to antagonize the player behind you but to buy you time so you don't have to trust in his driving skills. A driver that's a half second behind you means you need more time to react smoothly. Look, if you get pushed up on the car in front of you and you have to grab a big handful, then that scat for brains behind you is gonna turn you into the jelly in a PB&J. By increasing your space cushion to the front you're buying time for yourself and Mr. Rideyourass. Increasing that space cushion should be a gentle business—don't brake check them, just gently open the gap with the car in front of you. On the expressway, if your concern is to "not invite" someone into your lane, let it go. You want space: which is time, so if something does happen in front of you then you're not depending on Rideyourass's ability to brake or maneuver. *You* need to be in control of your ride. If someone slips in front of you, so what? You're not worried about winning a race and blocking an opponent, you're trying to keep your options open and buy yourself time. As long as you're flowing with traffic this isn't a big issue— someone looking for gap to go faster is usually going to drop in, see that things are no better in front of you, and then move out looking for a break and faster flow.

After you've built some cushion, you have a couple of options available; you can look to move to a slower moving lane if you're on the highway. On two lane blacktop when you have someone sniffing your tailpipe, and there is traffic in front, the foundational approach is the same. Get yourself some time and space. Look to see if you can pull over or wave the offender by. Do not be surprised if your tailgater resists repeated flagging to pass. You may flag him by, and he'll simply sit behind you, hypnotized by your taillight, following like a zombie—that means he probably isn't even aware he is following uncomfortably closely; he's just doing his usual thing.

Take a moment out on the highway sometime and start noticing how closely cars follow each other. In my experience the average following distance is about one second during peak hours and one and a half seconds during non-peak. Those kinds of times explain why folks run into the back of each other so dang often.

Where were we? Oh yeah, if you've got some cushion in front of you, and the person tailgating you is clearly not aggressive or angry or possessed by the devil then...well...I like to play Tailgatering. The first move in Tailgatering is "Swerve Practice." Yup, just what it sounds like: practice your swerves! Yes, you are right, this works better at lower speeds, and I wouldn't suggest it as a freeway activity but, jeepers, swerving around a manhole cover or other more "imaginary" objects is a wonderful way to awaken the sleeping tailgater. You'll know you're getting somewhere when he starts backing off. Let's face it, if you're flicking your bike around he should wake up and ask, "WTF?" and back off. If not, I might move up to "The Weave" which is just a steady weave using up all the lane that is available to me. The Swerve and The Weave are non-threatening behaviors. They don't aggressively mess with the pinhead behind you, they simply make him ask, "Is this guy on this bike drunk...and how close do I want to be to him?"

Yes. I mess with their heads; and yes, sometimes they never notice.

A key for me is to give myself some control over the situation. If you have ever played chess you know that sometimes you're on the offensive and others you are on the defensive. When riding, there's a couple of states we find ourselves in; just like chess there is being on offense and being on defense. Offense is when you're proactive. You may not be calling the shots, but you're actively engaged in trying to take control of the situation. This isn't a clash of the titans or smash-mouth football but it is *chess*. When you are being tailgated, then you start tailgatering—massaging the situation to your advantage, positioning your pieces, looking down the time line to bend events to your advantage. Tailgatering is about getting back into the driver's seat and not being driven from behind.

There's an important life lesson in this whole thing because most of us at some point figure that we've lost control of a situation. The metaphoric tailgater gets on our butts, and we concede control to the tailgater. For me? I manifested diabetes at age twenty-seven; full on, type one, insulin dependent diabetes. I thought that was the end of a lot of things. Diabetes was a ball and chain—actually more of a cell—it was the beginning of the part of my life that could have been defined by "I can't, I have diabetes." Diabetes was tailgating me. I started watching the mirror instead of watching the road ahead. I have since rectified the situation. Next summer the plan is to take a thirty day road trip, not because I have diabetes. but because I want to in spite of having diabetes;

which means I make adjustments. Making adjustments means *I* am in charge, not a stinking, faulty pancreas. Part of my body may have failed me but that doesn't mean I kow-tow to a disease. You may be getting tailgated but you can turn it around, take control and start tailgatering.

SPEEDING

I ride too fast. I'm usually running ten over the limit. Yes, I am a sinner. Look, I'm a "safety professional" but not a "lyin' sack of safety professional excrement." I feel dirty for telling you the truth; but hell, I'm going all in. Here's the deal: I usually run ten over and occasionally fifteen—because that's what I can afford. *Oh,* and I never speed in Oregon because it is too damned expensive. Fees in Oregon are like, a zillion dollars for ten miles per hour over and 100 zillion dollars for eleven miles per hour over. Pull a runner in Oregon, and I believe they make you sign the title over to the State on the spot and then put two behind your right ear.

Don't speed in Oregon. Don't say I didn't warn you. And wear your helmet in Oregon; they're serious about that, too.

Why do I speed? Why would I admit to speeding? Because that's what motorcycles seem to do well—hustle along at a brisk clip. I'm not here to glorify breaking the law; I want to find that place where I'm honest with myself and honest with you, without pointing fingers or calling names. If your blood pressure is going up, and the book is trembling in your hands right now, you might consider skipping ahead to another chapter—I'm not going to twist this at the end and abruptly prove that speeding is dangerous, immoral, enlarges the national debt, and encourages terrorism. I speed. You speed. We all speed on motorcycles. Maybe just for a moment between stoplights when there's another bike on the line next to you, or maybe for two hours running across that open, naked landscape we call Nevada; either way we all speed. If you're saying, "No, not me!" Good for you, lots of second trimester brides wear white, and politicians believe every lie they tell.

Me? I speed, and I'm OK with it. I'm so OK with it that getting pulled over doesn't freak me out. I was exceeding the posted and got spotted; and, well, why get pissed about it? Remember, getting pulled over is a ritual, and if you know the drill you can keep time. The first thing that happens when you get pulled over is the officer will generally ask you, "Do you know why I stopped you today?" This is an attempt to get a spontaneous admission of guilt. Think of the story they could tell at the station house: "So I ask and the guy looks at me and says, 'Is it because of the three kilos of heroin in my backpack? Because if it's not that then is it's because I've been killing, skinning, and eating local cats.' So I tazed him on the spot—on principle..."

I know what's going on. I know I'm caught, and the question is do I evade or do I admit? I confess to ten or fifteen over—that's what I can afford. Even if I'm running hotter than that—hey, I was speeding but I'm not stupid, and I have no need to piss off an officer by getting all defensive and combative. He knows, I know, why fight? Admit to an acceptable fine and start the negotiations. Being reasonable is usually met with obliging, getting rude is usually answered with a bigger fine.

True story: In 1983, I owned a Suzuki GS550E that was piped and jetted, running sticky tires, which I generally rode like the twenty-year-old hooligan that I was. This was my second street bike, and the one that taught me how to brake and corner. It had a sixteen front wheel and dual front disks with "dual opposing pistons," and you could ring it's neck to a (then) breathtaking 10,500 rpms. I was cruising in a 35 mph zone running about 48 (didn't want to bust 15 over) and I saw a sheriff coming the other way. Immediately I looked down, noted my speed (too much—fer sure), and then watched as he passed me, slammed on the binders, and started to turn around. There was a momentary calculation on whether or not to pull a runner. You know: How fast is he going? How fast am I going? risk versus reward...but running ain't worth it, and I simply found a reasonably wide spot in the road to pull over, stop, and wait.

An aside: I don't like getting lit up by an officer, and I've never had an officer turn on the siren. Don't blow smoke, you know when you're done—there's no doubt—you know you're done, and the only question is are you gonna make Officer Bob annoyed by making him turn on the siren? About the time the lights go on, I'm on the brakes and have my right turn signal fired up. No need to yell, "Officer, I know this dance. Put the tazer down; that red dot on my chest is making me nervous and my only plan is to comply."

The deputy was a nice guy, I got my helmet off and the registration and insurance card out. We ended up having a long conversation about bikes, and we actually ended up, both of us, leaning against the fender of his Dodge swapping stories and having a good ole time. Eventually he said, "Well, I'm gonna write you up for 45 in a 35." My internal response was, "But we're friends!" but I smiled and grunted and signed the ticket. Twenty-five years later I used the same technique on a deputy up in the canyon here in Idaho, and I walked away with a warning. The only difference was probably the gray in my beard.

When I get pulled over I'm compliant and honest. I recommend that path. Usually it works out—I end up with a warning or a diminished fine. See, officers know where the fines jump up, and if you're over that line and they like you, they will cut you a break and write you for a lower number. If you're a dick? If you call their mother a name? If you make snide comments about "making your quota" or "revenue generating" then expect to feel the full weight and wrath of the law. Wait. Is Crash telling us how to avoid or blunt tickets? Isn't he a safety guy? Aren't all safety guys safety fascists? Shouldn't he be telling us to pay our full fines and get what we deserve? Nope. Sweet talk the cops; they are normal people with a potentially crappy day going on. Be nice. Don't be a sucker, but don't be a prick either.

If I were to tell you that I never speed and you shouldn't either you'd just push me off as another safety hypocrite. See, I know that safety people speed. I ride with them, and brother, they don't go the speed limit. Get them out on a nice canyon road and they'll wick it up on their Goldwings and hogs and adventure tourers just like any normal bunch of guys and gals. Before you're a safety pro you're a rider. Riders like to ride, and riding means occasionally flying low.

I believe as riders we owe ourselves some basic honesty, because if we look at riding as a cake, it's often frosted in sweet, sweet lies we tell ourselves and each other. Those lies take a lot of different shapes, and some we like and some we don't. Some lies we spit out and some we chew. What am I talking about? Here's a lie you might embrace: "Everybody who speeds gets caught or pays the price some other way." No. They don't. Loads of punks with too much throttle hand get by with it day after day after day and in the end when they hang up their spurs they have no soiled driving record to show for it, no jail time, no kink-tailed sperm that will result in sterility—they'll be just fine for it. Here's another tasty lie riders and non-riders alike like to tell: "If you don't wear a helmet you'll end up a vegetable." The truth is there's gazillions of guys riding without helmets who will never "eat through a straw" or "wear diapers for the rest of their lives" or "end up destroyed and drooling in a wheelchair."

Motorcycling isn't like that. Those are tasty, hopeful lies designed to hide the fact that you can, to some extent, cheat fate. That's part of the thrill of riding—cheating the reaper, jumping the turnstile, knicking a candy bar! Yeah, you just did a stoplight drag on Main Street and guess what? You got away with it! Pretty cool. Or you just ran the canyon too fast, not stupid fast, but just fast enough that if Ponch or John had seen you they'd have spit out that ham sandwich and come after you ticket book in hand. Dodged it di'n't ya? Perhaps you survived the commute, riding in your Dockers instead of dedicated riding pants—isn't that supposed to end with you and a date with a wire brush in the emergency room? Di'n't. Winning! On every ride you cheat the ferryman a little bit! Or maybe you don't—but millions of riders don't die riding.

Be honest—you've ridden in tennis shoes and paid no price for it. It's a lottery. If your number comes up and you need that helmet you're not wearing—*ouch*. But your number may never come up.

A final thought here: I don't mind liars. There are all sorts of different lies folks tell. Generous lies: "Yes, that dress does look unique on you!" Hopeful lies: "I'm going to get some dedicated riding gear as soon as I get a little ahead." Convenient lies: "If you don't wear a helmet you will die." Sympathetic lies: "I know what you mean—I'll miss him too." (No, you don't but why tell the truth in that situation?) Heck, we're surrounded by lies and some taste good and others are told to hopefully save a life or safeguard someone's feelings, but let me say just this one more thing:

Nothing is more pathetic than lying to yourself. Know who and what you are. Accept it. Deal with it. You'll be happier. I'm outta here—I'm gonna go for ride—and have a good time.

LANE SPLITTING

If you're thinking about riding you've probably spent some time thinking about lane splitting. Occasionally you hear this behavior called "white lining," but I graduated high school in 1981 so when you say "white lining" all I can think of is cocaine and Studio 54, so I don't refer to it that way. My take on lane splitting goes like this:

Imagine you're eighteen or twenty years old, your parents are out of town, and you decide to have a party. Your best bud (who has a girlfriend) calls and tells you he's bringing his girl and one of her "friends," a girl you've never heard of before. So you ask, "Is she hot?" and he answers, "Yeah, and she's easy, too!" If you're eighteen then you quickly convince yourself that the Queen of Hot & Easy is coming over and tell me this, Bunkie, how could she not love *you*? If you're a male you know how this story ends, and it's not a Penthouse Forum letter. It's more "Bride of the Living Dead." She's annoying. Your pal lied to you to satisfy his girl and bring her...ah...visually challenged friend. There's name calling and recrimination and basically it's an unpleasant scene.

If you're thinking that riding a motorcycle means that your

bike is bringing its hot and easy friend "Lane Splitting" to the party then you are wrong.

First the warning signs, things your pal will say that seem too good to be true. Things like, "Dude, she's a model!" Which it turns out is true—she's a hand model, because that's her best attribute. Frankly, you'd rather gaze intently at her well manicured fingernails than try and figure out which of her eyes to look into; is it the one that's looking at you or the one looking over your shoulder you should gaze at?

Lane splitting comes with this lie: "It's legal in California!" Which it is not. It is *"permissible* if done in a safe and prudent manner." Look it up. Oh, go on and holler and shout, but while you're looking to see where it expressly says "you can't" look up the definition of "reckless driving" which is the "wanton disregard of the safety of yourself or others" and realize this: If you shoot between two cars that are traveling at 35 miles per hour and you're doing 60, you're driving recklessly. Ain't no judge gonna agree you "were well within your rights" and did the "safe and prudent" thing. "Safe and prudent" should be a warning alarm that she may be a model, but she's a shoe model.

In the spirit of full disclosure, I will admit I grew up in the San Francisco Bay Area, and yes, I lane split when I'm there on a bike. I particularly enjoy lane splitting at intersections. That simple act of slipping between lanes to the head of the line still brings a warm glow to a special part of my cold, dark heart. When I arrived in Idaho, I immediately called the Idaho State Police to see what their policy on lane splitting was. It was incredibly simple: "If we see you doing that, figure on being cited for reckless driving." 'Nuff said. Oh, and from the "Urban Legends" file—that law that allows air-cooled vehicles to use the emergency lane during a traffic jam? Can't find that one anywhere. You're better off just telling the officer, "Hey, it's air cooled and I didn't want to overheat," and see if he'll just let it go.

As a motorcycle instructor I've heard all kinds of curious and odd ideas, rumors, and flat out lies about lane splitting. If you've lived in a state that permits it you'll probably recognize the rules of thumb that the cops taught to me back in Cali.

1.   Never travel more than ten miles per hour faster than the traffic around you.

2.   Never split lanes if accompanying traffic is moving faster than 30 mph.

3.   If you are splitting to the head of lines at an intersection, and the light changes and traffic starts moving, feather yourself back in as quickly and politely as possible.

4.   Never split to the head of a turn lane or between two turn lanes.

5.   If you are at the head of the line, and the light goes green be *very* careful as you enter the intersection. The first in is the first hit by someone jamming it through on a stale yellow.

6.   If you're not comfortable doing it, don't.

What happens if you follow all those rules of thumb? Life will be perfect, and you'll never have a problem, right? It'll be Shambala and Utopia and the Playboy Mansion all rolled into one, with you blissfully zipping between cars like crazy-legged Tony Dorsett, yes? Wrong. Think more like OJ Simpson. You can still get pulled over and written up. Why? Because while not expressly *illegal*, it's not expressly *legal* either, and that reckless driving statute has lots of room for interpretation. Sorry. No guarantees. One man's prudent is another man's pandemonium. Tie that together with a profound misunderstanding of what your "rights" are and you're wearing an orange jumpsuit wondering which of your county jail-mates would make a good...um...companion. OK, maybe not; but, seriously, if you get a cite for lane splitting don't expect to jailhouse lawyer your way out of it. You're in a world of subjectivity that would be best served by a professional lawyer. Do not start a conversation with a cop or a judge with a line like, "A guy named Crash wrote in his book that..." Bad idea, if you're fighting for real, get a real fighter.

I teach high school students how to make television. It's alternately painful and rewarding. I have a saying I invoke about learning: "Sometimes you have to bump your head to learn to duck." This means that I let them make mistakes so they can learn from them. I also offer scenarios to them to challenge them so they can visualize bumping their heads without really doing it. Here's a scenario to give you a chance to *really* consider what's involved in lane splitting.

You're riding on a four lane freeway, and traffic begins to slow...and slow...and slow. Before you know it, traffic flow has dropped to thirty miles per hour and periodically slower. There is no High Occupancy Vehicle lane, and you left the house late. You decide to split a couple of miles up to an exit and get off the main and work the back streets. You slip between the number one and number two lanes, run it up to 40 and start hustling down the white line. (See how that sounds like a cocaine reference?) As you're lane splitting you're on and off the throttle a bit but are holding a good speed. Suddenly a minivan with a bumper sticker that says, "Soccer is better without keeping score!" starts to drift toward the car next to it. You can fit if you just hustle a bit, hit the horn, and...that van keeps coming. Suddenly you're ping-ponged between a van and a mid-sized sedan.

Absolutely terrible situation. Awful. Your bike is twisted and your left knee is seriously tweaked, and you're probably going for an ambulance ride. The cops show up. Here's the tricky part: Pretend you're the cop—an honest cop—not the kinda guy to make sh*t up and give out bogus tickets that reflect his opinion instead of the law. Who do you write up and what do you write them up for?

Stop and think about it and suppress your hopes and prejudices as a rider. Be serious. Who was in the wrong? Remember that you effectively struck a vehicle from behind. They didn't clip your rear tire as you slipped it by, you pounded it into their sliding door while they were legally inside their own lane. If you were driving a Five Series BMW, instead of riding a motorcycle, how would you write that ticket? Yeah, if a four door German luxury sedan driven by a commodities broker had just pulled that move, how would you react?

Allowing lane splitting at intersections makes sense to me; it helps with traffic flow and protects riders from getting rear ended at large urban interfaces. However, I can't tell you to do it and you'll be OK—there are rules, you know? If you decide you would like to lane split, then do it with your eyes wide open. In California it's permissible if done in a safe and prudent manner, what that means is up to the policeman who is watching you. Everywhere else it's probably straight out reckless driving.

Here's my two cents. If you're sitting around dreaming of getting a bike so you can lane split, once you're on the bike the world takes on a whole new texture as you realize how vulnerable you are. You may be selling yourself the idea that Lane Splitting is a supermodel but in reality supermodels are heck of a lot of work and can cost you dearly—so be careful what you wish for.

RIDING TWO UP

When you take a motorcycle training course, one of the first group activities is in the classroom and you do that "I am, I'm from, and I'm here to..." round the room thing. People take courses for differing reasons, and you hear a lot of different reasons for taking a course, but one that comes up surprisingly often is, "My wife and I, we've always wanted to ride to...(some wonderful location, a couple thousand miles away)." Often both spouses are there and two motorcycles are involved, but a shocking number of times the husband is taking the class and the plan is for a two up ride. Riding "two up" is just my regional dialect for taking a passenger. Some call it tandem, or pillion, or just "on the back;" there is a rather demeaning term for being a passenger on a motorcycle, but I'll avoid that in the interest of not offending half the planet.

You should think carefully before you start carrying passengers. Carrying a passenger is a tricky business, because it changes the weight distribution of the motorcycle, sometimes dramatically. A passenger can actually steer the bike underneath you. Most importantly, like the captain of a ship, *you're* responsible for the safety and welfare of your passenger. Riders should be comfortable riding by themselves in all situations before they take a passenger. By this I mean if you're gonna take a passenger somewhere, you should be comfortable in that environment yourself. If you're going cross country then you should be comfortable in all the conditions that path would take you through: city, highway, traffic, mountain, prairie, heat, cold, or rain. As the captain of your motorcycle you owe it to your passenger not to try and drag her or him up the learning curve with you.

Read this in the first person: If I am not comfortable and competent in traffic or rain or the canyon, I shouldn't drag an innocent passenger out into them with me. As a rider, hurting myself is one thing, hurting another is a whole different kettle of chili.

My most common passenger is the lovely and delightful Mrs. Crash. She is the love of my life, the mother of our children, and I can't imagine waking in the morning without knowing she's nearby. I feel a tremendous responsibility when I put her on the back of the bike and take her out. Remember, when you're putting someone on the back of your bike you're responsible for someone's mother, father, sister, brother, friend, or lover; so act according. Take your responsibility for human cargo seriously.

First things first, before you take a passenger out you need to have a chat. You should discuss his or her expectations, your expectations, and some basic craft....Oh screw it, here's a list:

1.	Where are we going, what are we doing? Yeah...are you riding to the bar for a tequila drinking contest or are you taking your passenger for a pleasure ride around the block because he or she has never been on a bike before?

2.	Gear—I humbly offer that passengers wear long sleeves, long pants, gloves, and a helmet. Remember, this isn't about *when* you crash but *if* you crash. Often, telling passengers that they need a set level of protection will give them time to think about and internalize what they're asking you to do and about the risks that are there. You're not looking to scare him or her off, you just want a fully informed passenger.

3.   Mounting—My rule is simple: I am first on, last off. I fold the footpegs down while the bike isn't running and I'm not on it. I show passengers where they will be putting their feet. I make sure they know, left foot on the left peg, hand on my shoulder if they need it, right leg over, sit. *Oh* and don't try to get on or off until I say so. I will tell you to get on. I will have both feet on the ground, be in neutral, front brake applied, and then I'll say, "Saddle up," or "Mount up," or "Get on," or "Shall we?" or "Ready? Then do it," or some other thing that I think is reasonably cool. Once a passenger is on the back I'll double check to make sure he or she is ready to go with a "Ready?" before I go anywhere.

4.   Touchy/Feely—Lots of bikes have handholds for passengers. Make sure your passenger knows where those are. I have had the situation where as I start a maneuver a startled, off-balance passenger grabs a big handful of my jacket to right themselves and avoid falling off. Make sure your pillion pal knows where the grab rails are. I have no problem with female or male riders holding onto my waist or hips, it connects them nicely to me. It also puts their hands in a position where they can put their hands on the gas tank during extreme braking— they can squeeze with their knees and brace on the tank.

5.   Steering—Passengers tend not to be riders. They can be afraid of things like...leaning, and they will actively fight your attempts to steer the motorcycle. The lovely Mrs. Crash is the best passenger I have ever had because she leans with me and doesn't fight me in turns. Because she enjoys carving things up, she actually looks over my inside shoulder during turns—over the left shoulder in left turns, over the right shoulder in right turns. That simple movement with me, not against me, creates a synergy that is absolutely amazing. At times I forget she's back there. A passenger who actively fights your lean and tries to make the bike stay or go upright can make your life a rolling nightmare. Talk with your passengers

and make sure they know to lean with you; this is vital to your success and their safety. Remind them, if you must, that single vehicle crashes account for almost 50% of rider fatalities and that means running wide, and running wide means not enough lean. Riding two up is a partnership, and either party can really screw things up. I watched a good friend on a mountain road with his daughter on the back, and she was just giving him hell fighting him—and he's a good, high-quality rider. I have been on the front fighting the passenger myself, and I'm here to tell you it's not a thing you want to do twice. Talk with your passenger about working with you.

6. Communication—If you can afford a two way communications system, go for it. If you can't then be ready to yell at each other. For stuff like "take a pee break" or "let's get some chow" I rely on the Holler & Hollerback system, and it works OK for me. Mrs. Crash and I also have a couple nonverbal cues we use for quick efficient comms. If I tap her knee once it's "Hey" and usually I'll then point at something I want her to see, a view or some kind of scenery. If I tap her knee twice (and this is a firm tap or even a slap) that means "Hang on." If I see something screwy going on in front of me, and I'm concerned I might need to take evasive action or brake seriously, I'll give her a heads-up double tap. If she wants me to see something usually she squeezes me and points it out. Because we don't have two way comms it's not unusual for us to be tapping and pointing a fair amount.

7. Dismounting—First on, last off. My rule for dismounting is pretty simple. When I turn the bike off, you're cleared to get off. Because I can stop, catch neutral, get both feet down, and then flip the kill switch without ever taking my hands off the bike, I like to let my passengers know that they aren't to go anywhere until the bike is shut down. Having a conversation before the ride helps ensure I don't have someone climbing off before I'm ready.

Passengers can make the ride a bit more challenging, but it also is a great way to share the riding experience. Mrs. Crash started riding dirtbikes as a teen and now has a motorcycle endorsement, yet she doesn't have a desire to be a rider—she likes to be a passenger. I enjoy chauffeuring her around, and we have a great time together. One thing we do occasionally is head out and have a quick practice session in a parking lot. I can practice starts and stops, figure 8s (helps with her body positioning), and a few U-turns. Yep, if there's a moderately complex move you might have to make on the road with a passenger it doesn't hurt to have practiced it once or twice in a safe, open environment.

Riding two up can be rather unsettling for people. If you've tried riding with someone on the back and you don't like it then don't do it. Going two up is a voluntary issue. You don't have to volunteer to be rider or passenger. Make sure you have a common set of ground rules when you head out and be sure to work as a team as you ride. Enjoying the company of a loved one or even just having a friend along for the ride can be a rewarding experience that brings you closer together, or it can be a kludge that puts you both at risk. The decision is yours.

Braking with a Passenger

I have been married twenty-four years. I still get a cheap thrill having the lovely Mrs. Crash press up against me. Call me a dirty old man, that's OK. One of the fastest and easiest ways to get that thrill is to go for a ride on the motorcycle with her as my passenger....and then brake like hell; cheap thrill, but thrilling none the less.

Riding with a passenger is a wonderful way to share your passion for riding. As opportunities go, you can give people a view into your world, help them understand what it is you love about riding, but, more importantly, you're sharing an intimate part of yourself in a close personal way—let's face it—when you've got a passenger on the back it's as close to a piggyback ride as it gets. Yes, we're all fifteen years old at heart, and since I've already introduced an element of sexuality to this, let's all get over it right now: Riding tandem can be kind of awkward because, well, you have to touch another human being. Don't believe me? Watch what happens when a male rider gives another male a ride.

Two guys on a bike is often called "riding mandem," a cute play on words and an attempt to make light of an awkward situation. How often have you seen two gentlemen on one bike? And if you did, and asked why, did you get an answer like "needed a ride back due to" loss of electrics, gas, flat tire, motor grenaded itself, you know what I'm talking about—mechanical failure. Last mandem ride I saw was after we had finished a ride up Bogus Basin Road in Boise. As we stopped at the bottom I noticed that the guy on the other supermoto was drooling oil all over the road. One of the drain plugs had dropped out. You want to see uncomfortable? Watch five or six guys trying to figure out who's giving the stranded guy a ride. Write it off to seventh grade gym class, or the fear of appearing "different," or maybe just the fear of being seen as the "weaker" or "less skilled" of a pair.

One of the unavoidable issues with passengers is the fact that you are in each other's intimate, personal space; hands are on hips, hips are inside thighs, helmets click together when you shift. If things go weird there's clutching and grabbing... Guys find that unsettling...well, with another guy...with a girl on the back, it ain't nothin'. Come on gentlemen, fess up, when you were eighteen and you had a bike, you always offered the pretty girls a ride—and your intentions were never to be an "ambassador for the sport."

The root of the issue is that with a passenger on the back any sudden input (throttle, brake, or steering) is going to roll that passenger around a tad. I don't care how talented your passenger is, how many thousands of miles they've put on, how long you've been a team—you can still startle your passenger with shocking ease. Think about the situation they're in! Perched on the back (often too narrow a seat) with their legs half way round the driver (knees often higher than their hips) and precious little to hold onto.

When I was fresh out of high school my friends and I would play a game called "Fighter Pilot." It was brutally simple and testosterone driven. Simply, you would get good and buzzed, then take a barstool and put it in the center of the floor (those barstools with the round foot on the bottom work best). Whoever felt they were the toughest would sit on the stool, grab the seat edge, and hold on as tight as possible. We would gather in a circle around the "pilot" and then simply pushed him over. You need to be in a tight circle because the idea is to catch him, then roll him to the left or the right or even flip him across the circle, where some poor fool would try catch him.

It was profoundly stupid behavior. (But funny as hell when you simply stepped out of the way and the "pilot" would have to try and eject or arrest his fall.)

Riding passenger is a little like playing "Fighter Pilot." You are a precariously perched passenger trying to keep up with what is going on. The rider knows what he's going to do next, but the passenger is simply getting a constant flow of potential surprises. Looking over the shoulder of the rider will help the passenger stay aware of what's out front but might not tell him or her what the rider is gonna do about all that stuff up there; is that blob-looking thing gonna require a lane position adjustment? Or maybe the pilot doesn't see it and there's a swerve coming. Where is braking going to start...or is that light stale and going yellow...either way are we slowing or going?

If you ride with a passenger then there is going to be a familiarity with "The Bump," meaning, on taking off, stopping, and shifting you often have the passenger bump into you. Depending on the style of ride you have, your passenger will occasionally bang into you. Helmets click together, shoulder blade meets chest, hips roll, and bodies collide. (Boy, that sounds kinda dirty...I like it!) Passengers get pinballed around back there. If you get hard on the brakes for an emergency stop, you're probably going to be wearing your passenger like a backpack.

Clamping on the binders causes the bike to pitch forward. On the back a passenger is then decelerating at a slower rate than the bike, and since the bike has dropped its nose, he or she is gonna come forward on the seat. Your passenger is going to bang into you, and you need to be aware it's going to happen. I like to communicate with Mrs. Crash by tapping on her leg or squeezing her knee; in an emergency braking situation there might not be time to give her a quick squeeze of warning. I'll be realistic, in some situations there is the opportunity to warn your passenger to be alert—a quick "heads-up"—but without voice communications your passenger isn't going to ever get much of a warning. An alert passenger maybe able to see a situation developing and prepare, but I wouldn't count on it.

Here's the average scenario for myself and Mrs. Crash: We're riding and something weird is happening, and I'm on the brakes. Mrs. Crash usually keeps her hands on or near my hips. Depending on the bike we're on she'll do one of two things; either reach forward and brace herself by putting her hands on the gas tank, or as she's pressed against me, she'll simply wrap her arms around me. As a rider I prefer when my passengers can brace themselves on the tank. It takes the weight off of me, and I feel more in control of the situation. (Well, having the lovely Mrs. Crash pressed up against me isn't a bad thing at all.) Either way if you have a passenger on back you need to be ready to carry that extra weight on your back.

As always, good communication before the ride is an excellent idea, as is a bit of practice in the parking lot. Remember, if you're practicing braking two up you're in a new and different situation: the bike is heavier, the passenger is a bit of a loose cannon, and things aren't going to be the same as when you're solo. Good technique always pays off, so keep your head and eyes up and remember that progressive squeeze on the lever; smooooooth is important in these sorts of things, especially since you're gonna have anywhere from 100 to 200 pounds of human using you as a backstop to keep from going over the nose. As always, if the front skids let it go and reapply. If the rear skids and stays in line with the front then release and reapply. If the rear skids and steps out big keep it locked.

Let me offer one more idea: Emergency braking with a passenger is going to feel heavy; you're gonna get slammed in the back; the bike will dive more than usual; it is a different experience than normal (just you) braking. If you're not willing to take a moment and prepare yourself for what braking with a passenger is like, then you probably shouldn't be taking passengers out for rides. Why? Because you owe it to them not to practice in the arena of the real world! Gonna take that neighborhood kid for a ride around the block? Nobody ever pulls out of their driveway in front of a bike right? Pretty girl at work wants to go around the parking lot on the back? Nothing bad ever happens in parking lots...

I'm not saying, "On every ride, with every passenger practice," but I am saying that if you're making a habit of traveling with a companion you should spend a few moments a month in a safe, controlled environment with a passenger practicing some of the things that will keep both of you alive; braking and swerving would be on the top of my list.

Turning Away

Warning—this is a "philosophical" piece...be forewarned. There comes a time when you become connected to your ride; a point when somewhere in your hips and groin you make a structural, spiritual link and suddenly with a strange common grace you *are* the motorcycle. It's hard to describe what it feels like when you realize that as your front tire strikes a line of paint—you feel it. Awareness of the suspension extending and compressing, the vibration that comes at 4,200 rpm and goes away at 4,400, or the deflection of the wheel on a crack or groove is a mystic, spiritual event that can consume you at times. Once you're in that zone there's no guarantee you're going to stay there; nor is there a warrant that you can't stay there all day. It is like a kiss; you're not sure how long it may last but you're blissful for the time you're there.

I've never had the monkey of addiction on my back and for that I am grateful. I've seen a few people struggle with dependence from a distance, and it's the sort of thing that has my sympathy and wakes me up to being non-judgmental. Clearly it is a heavy load, and I'm not gonna beat up someone with a 400 lb. monkey on his back. I do not intend to belittle those who suffer at the hands of truly nasty chemicals or organics, but I think that chasing the blissful moment of riding can become, if not addictive, a bit of a compulsion.

One of the main concerns of any religion or philosophy is helping people control their passions and appetites; whether it is the seven deadly sins or learning that "wanting" is the root of unhappiness, the idea that moderation and suppression of the self is in some way good is a pretty common theme. Not gonna argue any of that. I will proffer this: Riding can give you a spiritual/physical high, and that high is often fleeting and potentially intoxicating. If you wind up "chasing the buzz" you might find yourself in trouble.

Speeding is a buzz. Wheelies on Main Street? Buzz. Slapping a pass over the double yellow will buzz you up. I grew up in California and, yup, splitting traffic will give you a buzz.

For me, there is a fine line between "chasing the buzz" and having that spiritual connection where you're one with the machine. This is also where the religion stuff intersects— the idea that your passions and desires are natural, but you also need to subjugate those desires. Theoretically, most passions can be indulged in some form. For example, rather than being outlawed, sex is often given strict guidelines. Likewise, drinking may be acceptable but being a drunkard isn't. Eating meat OK, gluttony not so popular.

See where I'm going? Apparently I'm not the first person to realize that too much of a good thing can be a bad thing. You can have too much of good things. When it comes to bikes there are illegal activities which you can do on a motorcycle (which I admit I have done) that push you from having a nice bowl of ice cream to being a freaking pig. The real question is: How do you know when you're there? "The Line" is out there somewhere, and on a bike—what are the signs you are near or at it? I will grant that there are motorcycle interventions; times when friends or other riders try to step in and try to help, but as organized behaviors led by therapists, it just don't happen. Nobody sits down with a pre-written letter and six other friends and a licensed pro to talk a rider down off his wheelie habit—or maybe they do—I don't know. I've never been part of one. The intervention riders seem to get the most is from the friendly, well-intended, not-your-best-friend; you know, the guy at work, the lady in line at the 7/11—someone who you share little true friendship with—the kind of people who find you a target of opportunity to lay a "You know what they call motorcycle's down at the ER don't you? *Donor*cycles!" I honestly don't know what they think they're going to accomplish but I'll let them try—I'm kind that way, I can be very kind to people who are hawking religion at my door or telling me I'll die a gory death because they know someone who knew someone who once met someone who did.

This all goes back to what your mother told you: "If you run with scissors, you will put your eye out." Emphasis on the word *will*. Yes, I have run with scissors; and, yet, somehow still have stereo vision. You know why that is? Yup, you do, and if you're a "safety professional" like I am that causes some cognitive dissonance—see lots of safety education is built on the idea that "if you run with scissors you *will* put your eye out" when in fact, the reality is "if you run with scissors you *might* put your eye out," which really means: "You can run with scissors and not get hurt." All this falls back on any piece of well-intended advice from the slightly-known who give it: It's a not a rule, it's a warning, and in the attempt to make a warning stick with the warned we often embellish, and *might* becomes *will*, and a possibility is sold as a certainty.

Listen to how extremely odd and dangerous this feels: You can drink and ride and suffer no ill effects.

Wake up (I'm gently slapping your face), come on back, open your eyes, you're OK. Let's sit up, you might be a little dizzy. Shocking, yes? Here, have a drink of water. You're going to be alright—I believe you swooned. That's OK, I can barely say it because it's so damn foreign an idea; the problem is that, well, it's true. Every Friday and Saturday night countless hundreds (maybe thousands) of riders go out, ride to the bar, have a cold one or two and then ride to the next bar or back home suffering no consequence other than drinking sub-par beer.

How do you tell someone who rides to the bar every weekend that he's playing a dangerous game?

How do you tell someone who rides a wheelie down main street that he's also playing a dangerous game?

Got a serial speeder in your circle of riding buddies? He'll tell you it ain't grabbed him by the nuts yet, what's the problem?

This is where we come back to chasing the buzz. When I was young I chased the buzz—I did things because they were thrilling; your heart beats fast, you sweat, adrenaline courses through your brain, you get your buzz on. Nowdays busting out a wheelie or a stoppie is still buzzworthy but so is uploading a video I know is going to get 2,000 views in a week. Riding robustly and over the speed limit? Still a chill and deadly serious, yet reckless with reckless abandon. What turns your crank, melts your butter, stokes your engine?

Do not lie to me. Something tickles your pickle.

The question isn't what that thing is—the question is *what* drives the motorcycle? You or the thrill? In the throes of passion can you make like the Southern Pacific and pull out on time? Or are you trapped by the excitement? Can you walk away or does that voice in the back of your head or that tug at the back of your hips start pulling and you just... have...to...

Here's a story: I was up on top of a mountain loop that *lots* of riders use locally. As far as loops go, it's a *very* nice one; there's tight and technical, open and flowing—I would compare it to a good meal: it never fills you up on one thing, just moves between courses in a way that leaves you satisfied but not stuffed. Any good meal will have a bit of a pause in it where you get to cleanse your palate and ready yourself for what's next. This particular path has some very nice spots where you can pull over, relax, reflect, and ready yourself for the next section. Not so strangely, loops like this are often more difficult in one direction than the other. This one, the Lowman Loop, is more technical when you do it clockwise. Running clockwise you have to descend from Moores Creek Summit down into Idaho City. That descent is tricky with some hairpin turns. Run it counter-clockwise and you ascend those hairpins, and it's *much* more forgiving.

I was up on the other side of that summit one day, riding a 1992 Suzuki GSXR 1100, a big beast of a race replica bike that was famous for injuring professional racers at the Isle of Man road race. I was running the loop counter-clockwise and had paused to take off my helmet, check my blood sugars, and have an internal debate on whether to proceed around the loop or turn around and run the highly technical decent. In the distance I heard the familiar buzz of bikes running hard—you know, that cool sound that happens at around 10k—a part rattle, part scream, part pure smooth candy—the kind of sound a really good rock and roll singer makes, melodious and screeching all at once.

As that beautiful racket came closer I heard the exhausts popping and revving, and it became clear that these guys (and gals it turned out) were going to pull up and take a few moments where I was relaxing. Sure enough, in a moment I watched as five or six sportbikes rolled in and pulled up. Cooling engines were ticking and exhausts pinged, stainless steel contracted back to normal sizes, while the ritual of helmets and gloves coming off started. A mixed group, this was three or four guys and two young ladies. They were serious riders and were having a right proper motorcycle conversation. This wasn't: "Dude—I so rocked that!" or "You suck; I'm sooo much faster than you!"

This was a conversation with hands. Hands bladed up and

nipping and tucking and "hold the outside, then duck to the apex" and pitching the fingers down to show compressing the front suspension or dropping a wrist to show the bike crouching and firing out of the turn. Dear friends, these were fast people. The kind of people who, when I was twenty years old and living every Sunday all day up in the SF Bay Area on Highway 9 or 35 or 84, I would have peed myself with excitement to ride with.

Fast guys (and gals).

In the day, I would haunt (and hunt for) other riders on fast bikes, people to slot in behind and make the bikes twist and go. I was perfectly happy and it tickled my pickle to find a rider or group of riders and then drop in and start running with them. Running too fast, with people you don't know, who's skill set could be dreadful or spectacular was one of the ways I chased the buzz. Riding at big speed with people you've never met and have no idea of their abilities is a rush. You could get schooled or give a schooling; and that, friends, makes your heart beat faster, and is intoxicatingly exciting.

Sitting there, chatting up these serious folks and feeling that tug of the buzz, I had a curious internal struggle. Looking at tires I saw they were hot and starting to shed rubber in those odd little rolls. The front tire profile wasn't round, it was a pyramid—the sides were worn out, but the center was still good. Some were wearing full leathers, and the kneepucks were scuffed rather profoundly. (Meaning these folks got knee-down, and did it for real.)

Basically, everything about these people said, "We're fast."

And I wanted to be fast with them...and I didn't. I won't call this a junkie's lament or that fabled "bottoming out"— it was and it wasn't. I had in my head two clear voices: Buzzchaser and Brent. Folks will get nervous that I actually hear voices, and in some ways I do—ideas present themselves, and I understand they are complete thoughts coming from different parts of my psyche. I am now, and was then, no longer a young man. I will still do wheelies and stoppies. I ride too fast. I'm a knucklehead in traffic occasionally—but do I still have the stuff to reach into that dark box, close my hand on whatever's in there, and hope it ain't a snake? I want to...I really do...but once I start down this road, can I turn back? At what point are my teeth so deeply in that I can't let go, and I hang on too long, brake too late, ask for more traction than the road has?

Once I start drinking from that paper bag—can I stop before stupid happens?

Short answer? Nope. They asked me to join them. They were kind, serious, and nice people and I said no; I was going the other way. Everybody suited up and they left, toward the technical downhill run. I turned right. I turned away and don't regret it. I've gone for spirited rides since then and run hard, but my chasing the buzz days may be over. Stupid is still fun, but I think I know the difference between the thrill of doing it right and the thrill of survival. Yeah, I survived a lot of rides and they were thrilling because I survived them; the buzz was the hiss of disaster in my ear. Cheating death is a scintillating business and when you're young simply surviving certain behaviors is pretty dang fun. With age? The buzz comes off some things as the reality of the consequences comes into focus.

So what's the point, Crash? What are you trying to say?

I'm saying that as you look at your riding, there's a time to lean into the turn and there's a time to turn away. Honest self-evaluation is an important skill for a rider to have. Sure, you can walk up to a friend and tell him what an ass he is and how he is a danger to himself and others, but it's not gonna do any good until he's ready; and when he's ready to turn away, he will. And for you? Welcome to the club; the club where you get to watch and wait for someone you love to be ready to turn away.

PREJUDICE

Ever sit around in an airport? I get that chance once in a while. It's not like I'm in the airport every week, but I get a couple of flights a year and it turns out airports are an excellent place to see Air, Fire, and Water.

I was in the Minneapolis airport with the lovely Mrs. Crash, where we were waiting three hours to make a connection. Yes, I live in Idaho. And yes, you can get there from here but it's gonna take some doing. You're not going directly anywhere. It's doglegging through Minneapolis to get to Kansas City or doglegging through Phoenix to get to Orlando. Getting there from here can be a conundrum.

Those moments, both sitting in the airport and trying to book a flight to DC, are when you get to see Earth, Air, Fire, and Water.

On your bike you get that "idea," that itchin' to ride to Sturgis, or Laughlin, or Laguna Seca, and you start making a plan to get there—that's Earth. There's mapping, calendaring, getting the bike mechanically sound, deciding how long a day is too long a day, or how short a day you need so you can stop by the jellybean factory. Those Earth moments are usually private things. You, with a list, in the garage. In an airport people are putting those plans into action—the Air, Fire, and Water moments.

You see people in the Air on the way out; they *are* way out, excited, flush with the heady excitement of "I'm finally gonna do this, see that, or meet them." Soldiers going back out after the break at home following boot camp. College students going to school or off to that "trip of a lifetime." It's just a cool deal to look and see who's Air, who's Fire, and who's Water.

Children on the way to Disneyland? Air.

Family trying to make that 20 minute connection in Denver on the way to Disneyland? Fire.

Family on the way home from the "greatest place on earth"? Water.

You'll see the same thing in riders out on the highway. There's a definite difference between a rider on the front side of a five hundred mile day and one on the back side of a five hundred mile day; and an entirely different look on a guy who's used to doing five hundred mile days and is busting out three in a row, or going for seven-fifty 'cause he knows what he's doing.

Airport waiting can be tooth-grinding boredom. To me, if you're sitting in a terminal with your mind bleeding third grade afterschool memories into your forebrain to keep you entertained (Yes, I remember getting "called out after school" in third grade; meet by the back stop, bring a few buddies...), then you're in the Fire world. Personal suffering (or public) in the waiting area at the gate is a symbol of struggle, or unpreparedness, or simply having a plan that pancaked.

True story: I had just worked a game day show in Eugene, Oregon, and was flying back to Boise. I was with Brad, a good guy with whom I often work, and as usual, we had to go somewhere else to get to where we wanted to be. In this case it was San Francisco. On the way out to Eugene, I had made looking for fresh sourdough bread my time-killing event going through the San Francisco airport. That's not hard to find. It absolutely murdered the thirty minutes I needed to kill. I had fresh, delightful bread to nibble on while waiting for the flight to Eugene. On the return, we busted chop and tried to make an impossibly close connection so we could avoid a *long* wait. We failed and wound up spending four hours in the San Francisco airport.

I considered killing myself; because airports can be that much fun. We got some food from burger royalty. I texted the family. I was perusing the book stores and magazine stands. I was out of bullets in about forty-five minutes. I turned to Brad and said, "What now?"

"Easy," he said with a smile, "we'll go to the bar." See, in Crash World there are bars in airports, but I had never been in one, not once. I will go to the bar with business associates. I will order the fish and chips and a diet soda, but bars are not a destination for me. I don't walk down the street or the breezeway and think, "Wonder if there are any good bars around here where I can kill an hour or two?"

It turns out Brad knew about airport bars. Fortunately for us, Oregon/USC (which we had just shot the morning pre-game for) was on. We sat down, I ordered a diet soda and a sandwich, and we watched TV for three hours in the airport, in the bar.

It was great. I would have never, ever thought of doing that. It's just not an optional kind of thing for me. I am part of a religious tradition that eschews booze. As a young man, this required some experimentation to find out what the deal with booze was. Tell a teenager, "Don't do that," and they will. I had to go find out what the deal with alcohol was. I did. I understand it's value as social lube. I know what a good buzz feels like. I realize that too much of anything, whisky or ice cream, is probably a bad thing. Now, I just don't drink because me and the Big Guy have an understanding. Some folks don't eat pork; I skip the JD and still get to eat bacon. Good deal. In my religious tradition bars are *Fire*. You don't go into one, because all that happens is people get drunk and catch social diseases from persons who are not their spouses. Alcohol isn't inherently bad, but it can be used as an accelerant to act foolishly. The guy who cheated on his wife and blames the booze? The worst kind of liar because he had thought about it, played with the idea, put himself in the position to make it happen, and then blamed the tequila when it did.

That's the crap that leads a bar from being a place to socialize and kill an hour into a den of iniquity where "nothing good ever happens." Admission time: As I type this I'm oddly nervous about getting caught saying nice things about dens of iniquity. Yeah, and in the San Francisco airport I was nervous that someone from church might catch me hanging out in a bar. Bummer.

Simply put, I was in a bind in an airport, and Brad brought Water to the situation. I brought Fire; he brought Water. I was freaked out, and he had a *simple* fix I would never have considered.

The exact same thing happens all the time in the motorcycle world. Take dragging the rear brake when you're doing low speed maneuvering; it's a trick that law enforcement officers and MSF rider coaches know and use, but the average rider may be aware of it but is probably not actively using it. That's OK though, it's a skill that you'll find written about, discussed in training, or shared privately; but as a skill that is self-evident? Not so much. People don't just suddenly say, "I know! I'll drag the rear brake and that will tighten up the bike and help with slow speed maneuvers."

Riders find themselves in a tight spot (Fire) in places like parking lots, dead ends, any situation where they look and say, "I can't turn this thing around here."

They may have a eureka moment when they decide to use the rear instead of the front to slow in a tight spot, but realistically, just discovering the rear and it's ability to stabilize a slow moving bike isn't going to be a discovery moment. Dragging the rear is most likely gonna be shared knowledge; a tip passed to you by someone you respect.

Among some accomplished riders dragging the rear brake is considered...well...lazy and poor technique. I've heard motor officers chide each other about being "one of those guys who drags the rear." Why do they do that? Because you don't have to drag the rear, if you're perfect from the word *go*. If you enter a pattern or turn at the right speed then slowing isn't an issue. You start correctly, you execute correctly, and you leave correctly. There's an exercise called the "in and out box," which is basically about eight U-turns in a row with an eighteen foot circle at the end. If you're a little warm into that box, you've got to adjust your speed, and the best way to do that is drag the rear a little. Byproduct? The bike is a little tighter and easier to handle. Downside? You might get into the habit of *always* using the rear brake, which isn't a bad habit—just a bit of a crutch.

When Brad suggested we go to the bar to kill time at the airport, my first instinct was that bars are for drinking. I had forgotten that bars are for socializing and relaxing. My preconceived notion of bars was simple and bound in religious culture. Functionally, there are groups of people out there who believe the only thing a bar is good for is getting drunk or cheating on your wife or plotting to kill the governor. There, straight out, there's a bit of a potential prejudice against bars amongst religious-minded folks. The rear brake gets the same deal. I grew up riding dirtbikes where the rear brake is your friend. Dirtbikers "steer with the rear," often locking the rear wheel and changing direction with it. I then went to street bikes, and sportbikes in particular. Sportbike riders will tell you that using the rear brake will kill you. (Cruiser riders on the other hand are prejudiced against the front brake, but that's another story.) Once a behavior or tool becomes in some way taboo or frowned upon we tend to not be willing to use it. We take a tool out of our toolbox because one of the *potential* uses is considered illicit or potentially dangerous.

The lesson here is to remember that just because something can be used inappropriately doesn't mean that thing is useless or should be avoided. I've run into sportbike riders who have removed their rear brake because "it's just dead weight that wants to kill you." That's just dumb. There's a reason that MotoGP bikes, the most technologically advanced, fastest bikes in the world, are all still sporting rear brakes. Likewise, there's a reason there are bars in airports. My problem was that I had forgotten that bars, like brakes, are subject to irrational prejudice. We killed three or four hours in that bar. We drank no alcohol. We had fun, it made my life better and easier.

Just like dragging the rear, it's a tool I'll use again.

WHY?

For some of us there never was a "Should I buy a bike?" moment. I can only speak for myself in saying for me it was always something I wanted at a visceral level; it was in my bones and my heart. I never questioned if it was economical, or reasonable, or smart. I just wanted it so damn bad that I didn't dare speak of it to my parents until I had the cash to buy one, by then I was seventeen, and they said, "No, absolutely not."

"No" bounced right off me. It didn't shove a red hot poker into my soul or crush me in any way; I simply thought "this is gonna take some more doing." My pop was a big fan of the "once you're eighteen" philosophy. I knew that once I turned eighteen several things changed. First, if I wasn't in school I would have to pay rent. Second, if I wanted a car to drive I had to come up with one. Third, if I needed bail, don't waste that one phone call dialing home. I figured at eighteen, all bets were off, and they were. I bought a 1978 Honda XL500S and brought it home. Only thing my pop said was, "Here's the name of my insurance agent," handed me a phone number and offered: "You'll need PD and PL, property damage and public liability. After that, you might want medical for passengers, unless you don't plan on carrying any. My insurance will cover you pretty well." Pop was an engineer, he had a very low Hewlett-Packard ID number, and he was serious about letting me carry my own weight but was also willing to help.

Pop never asked me *why* I wanted to ride. I never asked him why he loved planning and making things. (He was valedictorian of the College of Engineering at Utah State University.) After he passed away, I was removing a saw from his workshop to move to mine and when I finally got it out I found, drawn on the counter it was mounted on, the blueprint pop had drawn in preparation to setting it—engineer's plans with measurements and diameters for where the holes were to be drilled.

Why? It's a tough question. It's the reason we seek and sort through religions trying to figure out "Why am I alive?" or "Why do bad things happen to good people?" There's that classic image of a broken man, on his knees, clothes in tatters, rain falling, and shaking his puny, dirty fist at the sky shouting, "*Why?*" It's a tough question. The motorcycling "why" question often comes from those who don't ride.

"Why do you ride that thing?" is a question I've been asked probably hundreds of times. Thinking about it, I don't think I've ever had a lot of riders ask me, "Why do you ride that thing?" People at gas stations ask. Students at school ask. Folks at church ask. Friends, firemen, and farmers have asked. I can't remember any other riders asking, which is probably what has helped me formulate my answer to those well-meaning, interested people who do ask, "Why?"

I say, "Why not?" Stick that in your hookah and smoke it; how come you don't get it? Yes, it's rude and, yes, sometimes folks get flustered, but in all honesty what frickity frackity fudge am I supposed to be able to do—put you into my soul for a moment and make you feel the "why"? Why do I love the delightful Mrs. Crash; how do you put that into words? Platitudes can be rustled up pretty easily, but how can I honestly express to you the depth of emotion, connection, and love I have for her? She is the other half of me, and I cannot imagine her not being there. Why do I love her? *Why not?* What's not to love? Sure, there are times we don't get along and that's natural, but that discord is easily patched. I just love that woman. Students in my high school class are amazed that we've been married over twenty-three years. Given the state of many of these kids' families it's not surprising they ask me, "How did you know it was *Love?*" I often tell them I knew it was love because it was different than when I was a teenager. Teen girls don't like that answer.

In some way, we owe folks some kind of reasoned answer to that eternal question, "Why do you ride that thing?" You *are* going to be asked why someday; it may be at the family reunion or in the company lunchroom, it could be an uncle or cousin, or any number of people on the periphery of your life, but that question is out there waiting for you. If you haven't been asked yet, you will be. If you have been asked you may have formulated a pat answer. In the spirit of helping a rider out, here are my three favorite answers other than, "Why not?" Feel free to borrow them if you need them.

1. "It's fun." Simple. It is fun, yes? Who can argue with having fun? There is lightness in riding, you are more closely connected to the machine, the environment, and your own skills. It's fun to be in control, in the elements, and to be part of the machine.

2. "They Get Decent MPG." Yup, depending on the ride, you're gonna get anywhere from 35 mpg to 120 mpg. You can say 35 mpg ain't that good, but hitch the mileage with "It's fun" and, well, in my mind it's a good argument. When the price of gas spiked there was a corresponding spike in interest in motorcycles and motorcycle training, so to my mind it's pretty clear that if you're looking for an excuse to ride, MPG fits the bill.

3. "The devil makes me do it." Call him what you may— Satan, Beelzebub, Ol' Scratch—I go for the easy answer and

blame the Dark Lord. People are surprisingly accepting of this answer. It may be that the entertainment industry has primed them for embracing the idea that bikes are the devil's underpants, or it may be they realize that "The devil makes me do it" is actually a deflection—an "Oh! Look! Shiny things!" kind of answer that says, "Don't ask, it's hard to explain. I'm not offended, it's just difficult."

We all ride for the same reason: we like it. If we didn't like it we'd stop doing it. When I was a youth pastor I used to tell young men that kissing a girl wasn't like sticking a fork in your thigh; kissing is *much* more fun and that's why all their friends picked hanging out with a girlfriend, over hanging out with male friends. If kissing was like sticking a fork in your thigh, you'd do it once and then never again, and men would never have to say things like: "Bros before...um...girls."

For some, riding may be like jamming a fork into a meaty part of your own body—if it is, don't ride. For me, riding is a longing that when filled is deliciously absorbing; it's the rush of a gasping breath after submersion; it's seeing Mrs. Crash after a weeks separation—I cannot imagine living without it.

EARPLUGS

Wear them. If you don't you're an idiot. Was that too strong? I'll be honest, you're really not an idiot if you don't wear earplugs, but I'm here to tell you *I* was an idiot for not starting sooner. Now I wear soft foam plugs that cut the ambient sound around me down about thirty decibels. I do it for a couple reasons: first, to safeguard what's left of my hearing, and secondly, to allow me to better concentrate on the business at hand. Oh, and thirdly, to combat riding fatigue.

Ted Nugent was not kind to my hearing. He had his way with my ears at the Cow Palace and the Oakland Coliseum Arena. Consensual it was, but somewhere in that haze and hammer I believe I left the top 5-10k of my hearing behind. Ted isn't the only suspect; it could have been any number of late '70s, early '80s hard rock groups, but I believe Ted is probably man enough to own his amps and say, "Yeah, we were that loud, and you liked it that way," and not get all touchy-feely lawyered up. It was *supposed* to be loud. It was loud and my ears rang for a couple weeks. I am cool with that. What I am not cool with is getting off my bike and having my head ring and having to ask, "Say it again—louder," to people because the wind blast and exhaust note have beat my eardrums dull with that blind white-noise roar we find in our ears when we ride.

Doing some quick research I found said that even inside a helmet the noise can be over 105 db. That's loud enough that if your boss exposed you to it, OHSA would have his ass for not providing you hearing protection. It's loud enough in your helmet to hurt you. *Motorcycle Consumer News* is an excellent resource for more information on this issue.

As I said, I recognize three distinct benefits (unless I think of a fourth by the end of the page) they are:

1. Concentration. With the wind blast cut down I can actually focus better on the world around me. The cacophony of wind noise covers up sounds I want to hear. I end up trying to listen through the noise to hear sounds I want to hear. Without earplugs, I cannot hear subtle engine sounds at all, only wind, exhaust, and induction. There are things I want to hear besides the exhaust note; things like the valve train and cams, pre-ignition (if it's happening), and just the overall mechanical soundness of the engine. Rather than *trying* to hear, I can simply hear and that frees my mind for other processing issues. Here, try this at home: Get your favorite gonzo album and play it *really* loud as you're trying to type an e-mail and see how that feels. Next, same album, volume down to where you can hear other people speak—feel the difference in your mental acuity and ability to process?

2. Long term hearing conservation. Your hearing deteriorates naturally over time. If you're over thirty years old, odds are you can no longer hear the "mosquito tone" that kids use on their cell phones. The mosquito tone is a tone above 13 or 14 Khz that most people over thirty can't hear—because of age and abuse—OK? Kids use it on their phones in classrooms because we adults cannot hear them ring. True story: I had a kid in my high school class who thought it was hilarious that I couldn't hear it, so he'd play it all the time and kids would snicker...until I downloaded it and played it

at what was apparently (I didn't hear it) a tremendously loud volume. Hands flew up and covered ears. I stopped it and said, "I can do this all day—are we done now?" at which point the mosquito ceased to be an issue in my room. I've read that some convenience stores will use it to drive out teens who are hanging around. All this demonstrates the idea that your hearing naturally decays, and you shouldn't be doing things to accelerate it. There was one kid in the class who deafly sat there and then said, "Why can't I hear it?" It's probably that personal music device he has wedged in his ears all day...but the music isn't as good as Ted...

3.   Fatigue. A day on the bike can beat you down and sound does contribute to it. I was shocked by the difference I physically felt after riding with the plugs in; I just felt better. I assume this is a psychological effect and is all in my head, but I'm not as battered and beaten. In short, I just feel better after riding with plugs.

One thing that will impair your ability to hear is tinnitus, or ringing in your ears, which is caused by (You know what I'm going to say, right?) loud noises. So, riding an obnoxiously loud bike can leave you with hearing loss and ringing in your ears—because unlike the neighbors who get a break from your loud bike—you travel with the sound.

People often complain that plugs do things like create a situation where you can't hear emergency vehicles or other important sounds. To this I say, "Phooey." Why? Because all that the plugs do is cut down the amount of noise, they don't selectively remove sirens or horns, they mute the sound, not remove it. Are earplugs cool? Heck no. Watch people get grumpy as you roll them and put 'em in. You might get called a wimp, but at least you'll hear what they're saying. As far as arguments go, I wouldn't argue that "I've heard..." on this issue; try it out for yourself. Get a pair, stick them in, ride; take them out and ride some more; see if you don't feel a difference. What have you got to lose?

TWILIGHT

No. Not the books or the movies. Haven't read them, haven't seen them, just know that I can no longer talk about that time when the sun is setting and it's still light unless I call it "dusk," which although an excellent descriptor is not often used in the American lexicon. I want to talk about dusk and dawn in this chapter.

Dusk and dawn bring a unique set of problems for riders, the first of which is visibility. The sun is low and drivers can be blinded by it, and cars can be harder to see if they delay turning on their headlights. I'm pointing at two separate issues here: being blinded by the low sun and working in a low light environment. As riders, we know that other users can have a hard time spotting us. Imagine how hard that can be for drivers squinting into a rising or setting sun. *Hey!* Think about how hard it is for you on your bike when you're ducking and tilting your head trying to get some shade for your eyes at six in morning, when you're riding into the rising sun. If other users can barely see, then they will definitely have trouble seeing you.

By federal law, bikes have constantly burning headlights, which helps make you a little more visible in this situation. Cars, on the other hand, have on and off switches for their headlights and guess what? Drivers often delay turning them on until they need them. If the sun is low and in your eyes you need to realize that car drivers probably will *not* have their headlights on, particularly around dusk when they've been running all day without lights. (Dawn may be a different issue because a car starting a journey in darkness may still have lights on.) A driver blinded by the sun on the horizon is dangerous to riders. If the sun is at your back, you need to remember that you are harder to spot. If it is in your face, you need to remember that your vision is impaired. In either case, you need be especially attentive to your surroundings and other users.

We get awful worried about left-turners violating our right of way, and that's a reasonable fear; now imagine that left -turning vehicle facing into the setting or rising sun! But the problem isn't always *them,* sometimes *we* can be a contributing part of the problem. A motorcycle left-turning out of the sun across another user's path is in a particularly dangerous position; early in the morning and late in the afternoon we need to be aware of the sun's position as we ride. Where is it? Where are we? What is the geometry of my situation with other users? Remember "Black Sheep Squadron"? (If you don't that is too bad—great show.) In that TV show the premium dogfight started with someone diving out of the sun at his surprised opponent. Why out of the sun? Because you can't see something coming out of the sun! Like a bike, or a semi, or a Japanese Zero, or Pappy Boyington and his ragtag band of heroic misfits.

Vision and visibility are obvious problems when you're staring into the sun; well vision is, visibility can easily be overlooked. There's an important lesson in that: if you're having trouble seeing, then you're also having trouble being seen! Yup, Nanna was right: what's good for the goose is good for the gander. Speaking of animals, dawn and dusk is a time when animals can be more active. Deer, elk, and other wild animals will come out in the cool of the morning or evening to forage. Likewise, you'll find insects to be more active in the cool parts of the day. Hitting a deer is easier if his flying insect buddies have covered your visor in a Technicolor slather of bug guts. Yup, there's an entire animated movie in that idea, isn't there?—Billy offends the animal kingdom, so one day he's out on his ride, and all the bugs kill themselves by crashing into his visor. (They don't die though—kids' movie—they poop and puke.) As the visor gets covered up, bug poop and vomit gets into his lid. He starts freaking out, looks up, and there's a half dozen deer and yaks standing in the road...pooping (kids' comedy). Billy grabs a big handful, locks the front, tucks it, gets pitched off, and slides into a giant pile of bear poo. Billy is being loaded into the ambulance, and a singing bluebird lands on his head and (you guessed it) poops right between his eyes. Very green, kid-friendly, box office dynamite, yes? Wait! We could make him a billionaire industrialist, and he could be a gross carbon polluter and then change his ways and start building motorcycles that run on deer poop! This is money waiting to be made people!—

What was I talking about?

Oh, yeah, dusk and dawn cause problems with vision, visibility, and animals. Often in the dawn and dusk I will wear a retro-reflective vest to up my visibility. Yes, the sun is dangerous when it's low, but once it's down we tend to think, "It's still light!" when, in fact, it's getting dark. That little bit of trickery that we play on ourselves is the first step in forgetting that in the half-darkness of dusk or dawn our bright shiny headlights aren't beacons in the night yet but are still just part of the landscape. I mean this: If you're treating half-darkness as full light why shouldn't anyone else? Yeah, they're not worried about looking for headlights because it's daylight, right? Yeah, the problem is the same as impairment—you convince yourself that you're seeing the upside and not the downside; it's still day when in fact it's night.

I often find that I forget it's getting dusky until the bugs start up for real. Once I'm in bug city I'll actually think to myself,

"Where did all these bugs come from?" And instantly answer myself, "It's getting to be twilight!" At which point I realize— it's going to be dark soon and I should pull over and swap out of my tinted visor. Yeah, I'll ride 'til it's full-on dark without changing visors unless something like massive bug kills remind me of the time of day. Pay attention next time you're out at six in the morning or seven in the evening and the sun is over the horizon. I think you'll be surprised by how many other users are toodling around with their lights off.

Nobody's perfect—I think that we can agree on that one. So don't be surprised when people aren't. Likewise, don't beat yourself up if you're not perfect! The issue is that when we get into a low visibility situation, we get all freaked and nervous— but dusk and dawn are medium visibility situations, and that means we should probably err on the side of caution. It's better to be too visible in a medium visibility environment than it is to be not visible enough. Here's an example I think you'll relate too: fuel. Ever find yourself in a situation where you're sort of low on gas? You know, you'll probably have enough, or you'll be able to get there but have to remember to refuel before you go anywhere else. You could stop at that station two miles ahead but pressing on twenty more will get you to the destination, but you'll be a little low in the morning.

Don't lie...well, you can lie to me but don't lie to yourself; you've done the "This is gonna be a little tight but no big deal" thing. And you've pulled in and the next morning you say "What a great day! I should get on the road before it gets too dang hot!" Then, after you leave town, you suddenly realize that—oops—you're running low on fuel almost immediately. If you're lucky, you're not in a bind. But what you did isn't so uncommon. You passed a chance to get fuel, and it almost bit you. Likewise, don't pass up a chance to be visible at dusk and dawn!

Why Not?

When asked why I ride, I often answer, "Why not?" It's always fun to answer a question with a question to catch someone out, to punch when they're expecting weave, but I believe, "Why not?" is a reasonable and responsible question. As such, I have a few good reasons why you might consider *not* riding.

1. You are truly risk-adverse. If you end up with fear clinging to your back every time you go outside, if you are constantly worried that a stray strawberry seed caught between your teeth might lead to some kind of ghastly oral cancer, it might be a good reason not to ride. Riding is dangerous and if you're the type of person looking for absolute safety then you're not going to enjoy riding. Why? See number two.

2. Because, sometimes you just get screwed (and I'm not talking the good kind). As riders, we don't talk about this much, but there are crashes and deaths out there that just happen. I am a proponent of training, of alert riding, of riding within your limits, but there are times, rare times, when riders just get screwed. This is a subject we avoid; it's

the elephant in the room we all ignore. When that driver launches into traffic to fill that gap—and the gap turns out to be you—there are times you can't do a damn thing. Sure, we talk a bunch about planning ahead and situational awareness and that kind of thing, and we pretend you can anticipate everything, but that's a hopeful lie. Crap happens and occasionally someone gets blindsided. There, I said it. If you're not comfortable with the idea that you might take it in the shorts and that's just the way it is (even though odds are you will not get creamed), and if the possibility is too much for you; don't ride.

3. Health and ability. Ever watch road racing? I wanted to be a road racer, but God wasn't in on the plan. By the time I was eighteen and riding I was six feet tall and 198 lbs.—and back then I wasn't well-padded like I am now. Even if I had poured my cash into it, I was too dang big to seriously consider my dream career of racing. Now, I have Type 1 diabetes and I'm nearly fifty. For some, that means that the risks of riding have gone up dramatically; not only do I have to manage traffic and the machine, I also have to manage my diabetes; keep my sugars under control, remember that I become impaired for *many* new and exciting reasons. My age plays into things now—I'm not too old to ride, but I am old enough to know that if I fall it's gonna take some time to get back into shape. Age means I don't bounce as well, and diabetes means I will heal even slower. There are countless other physical issues that might preclude you from riding or create a situation that if you want to ride you're gonna *really* have to want it and work at it. Riding is a physically and mentally taxing adventure, and if there are limiting issues in your life that are more than you can manage, riding might not be for you.

4. Mental and physical acuity. How's that for dancing 'round the fire? You may not have "The Stuff." Yeah, some people can't play piano...at all; they botch up "Chopsticks." There's an outside possibility that you may lack the

coordination and skills to ride a bike. Look, there are just some people out there who are not riders. They aren't bad people. They just lack some circuitry or ability that they need. When I started training new riders, the older instructors would talk about running into someone who "couldn't turn right." Investigation showed me that, yes, a majority of people seem to prefer lefts, but this was the idea that there are people out there who *cannot* turn to the right. Which I put down to instructor legend and lore. Until I ran into someone who couldn't turn right. In the old curriculum we used to teach, students would turn left for the first three or four exercises before having to make their first right turns. I was enjoying watching, coaching, and counting noses when suddenly I realized we were short one rider. I looked around and found that outside my area of observational responsibility one rider was about to ride off the range in a strange arcing line. Immediately, I blew my whistle to stop everyone in place. All my little sheep (including the lost one) stopped. Long story short: We tried everything we could to get this poor person to turn to the right. We took a break and did one-on-one remediation. We tried helping with the head turn. We begged. We cajoled. This poor rider just couldn't turn right. It still ranks as one of the strangest things I've ever seen. There was a flash of anger (not shared) that I had because I thought this person was just dicking with us. Not the case. Amid tears of frustration this was the first person to whom I've ever had to say, "This might not be for you." It broke his and our hearts. It happens. Some folks just don't have it.

5. (And last) Age. This is one that offends and upsets people, so let me say straight out, there is no set age when you're too old to ride. It's a personal decision only you can make. Honest self-critique is difficult. There are plenty of people who want to put a fixed bar and say, "Beyond this age: *No.*" That is the easy way out, and I won't take it; I

prefer to put it on the rider. Motorcycling is a tremendously personal behavior. You may ride with a passenger, but in the end it's about you and the machine. As a rider, you have a responsibility to know your limits: limit of speed, limits of skill, limits of endurance, and limits of age. As much as I want to chase a faster rider on a road, I know it's a matter of personal responsibility to be able to say, "I'm in over my head," and I need to be able to shut the throttle and walk away. Pride can make bad decisions for you; pride will put you in places you can't get out of and holes you can't dig out of; pride goes before the fall. If you've reached an age where you're behind the curve, where you are constantly surprised by things around you, where you can't react as fast as you need to or mentally run with that pack of wild dogs we call traffic, then it's time to retire. When is that? I don't know—usually you're only sure after you've crossed the line and proven you were. How old is too old? That is on you.

Personal thought here: I was just out on the motorcycle range with a couple folks who might not be riders. Unless they become a danger to themselves or others they get to keep on training. Once that training cycle is complete, I know I will tell one that perhaps a scooter might be the way to go—with a scooter you don't have to shift, you can take that huge part of your brain's processing power and redirect it from looking at you hands and trying to shift and start paying attention to what's in front of you. Yes, there are work-arounds, you can ride a scooter or a trike of some kind; but the bottom line for me is that not all people are cut out to ride—if you fear you're one—then you probably are.

AFTERWORD

SUBMISSION

Some very kind, very moral, very uptight—I mean upright—people have warned me that I am going to hell because of the way I think and the way I ride. Not only do I speed, jump the curb, occasionally wheelie and stoppie in public, I cuss. Yeah, I drove trucks so I can cuss...oh, and I like to watch mixed martial arts (MMA) fighting on TV. If you find that repugnant, uncivilized, or just disgusting, socially-accepted violence then I apologize and promise not to spend too much time talking cauliflower ear, broken bones, dislocated appendages, or other physical mayhem. I am going to spend a moment or two talking about the concept of submission. In MMA fighting your goal is to knock your opponent out or to make him submit; that is how you win. Submitting is commonly called "tapping out"—the person who submits taps the mat, or just about anything he can reach, signaling his surrender; basically he cries, "Uncle!" The truth of the matter is that in a real bind a fighter can tap out or pass out—or worse yet—suffer grievous personal injury. Yeah, submit or have your elbow turned inside out or your knee twisted into a pretzel; it is a vicious business. Not your thing? Not a fan of watching two guys beat each other to bloody exhaustion? That's OK. Your revulsion will probably help make sense of the subject I'm about to discuss with you.

In MMA fighting, the concept of subduing your opponent is all about skill, strength, and domination. You need to put him into a situation where you can physically slam the door on his head...then you start slamming the door until he says, "Enough." It is just that simple. In the submission game the goal is to make it perfectly clear that you are about to fold, spindle, and mutilate your enemy until, if he doesn't tap out, he certainly will be going to sleep or perhaps looking at a long and painful rehabilitation. Watching two fighters maneuver, wrestle, and fight for control can be alternately thrilling and boring. Yeah, there's a point where two sweaty guys locked in an embrace on the floor grunting is...sorta...not attractive. Other times it is a gladiatorial battle of epic proportions. Watching two skilled guys is pretty cool, watching two unskilled guys is pretty sad.

Unfortunately, there are riders out there who ride their motorcycles with the goal of making the bike submit. Out there, on the asphalt and whining on the Internet, there is a type of rider, a school of thought, that believes you make the bike submit to you and your will. You've seen it. You may have even suffered from the first pangs of the dark hunger of "being a better rider" through "control" and "technique." A siren call of "Just do it exactly like this," and you'll have some kind of perfect ride or perfect corner or some sort of twisted orgy of immaculate, skillful riding that will take you to an altered state of super-riderdom. Tempting as it is to believe that, if you just learn the notes, the proper finger positions, practice the scales enough and *presto*—you'll be a virtuoso—I disagree. Submission in the motorcycle world flows the other way. *You* must submit to the motorcycle if you want to ride it well. Yes, in a sense, you have to tap out—admit that it's the thing that has you in a rear naked choke and start working with it, instead of fighting against it.

Ever try to drive a nail with a screwdriver? Or maybe you've tried to unscrew something with a pair of pliers. The fact is you can use the wrong tool for the job, and often you can get the job done, but the result is you end up butchering stuff and whatever you were installing or removing is essentially destroyed. But you can do it. So you say, go get the right tool, find the right device, and do the job right. Exactly...but in riding the issue is different because you only have one tool—*you*—what do you want to do with it? More importantly, what can it do?

When I talk about submitting to the machine, I honestly mean you submit to it. There are lots and lots of things any particular bike is capable of and plenty things it won't do. The first step in submitting to the bike comes with understanding what the bike's possibilities are. Don't focus on your shortcomings; recognize the bike's abilities. For example, the average in-line, four-cylinder sportbike will rev anywhere from 10,000 rpms to 14,000 rpms. Do you know why? Because that's where the horsepower lives. That's where the front suspension unloads and the handlebars waggle because the front wheel has gently left the ground in a power wheelie. Up there at the redline is where the ponies run wild and the really savage power lives, time warps and blurs, the landscape gets liquid, and sound stops because it is so damn loud in your helmet. A quivering, snarling sportbike at redline in third or fourth or fifth gear is in a place where Olympian struggles happen—that's one of the reasons you don't want a big sportbike for newbies—because when the power comes on up there it's a fine line between control and crash, expert or idiot, glory or goat. Most motorcycles never live to their full potential because up there in the thin air of total performance it's the rider who usually fails the bike.

Have you ever been there? Odds are no; because up there in the stratosphere of revs and power the air is pretty thin; and when—if you're there and don't know what you're doing—you try to make the bike bend to your will, the bike will instead bend you to its will. A fool's mistake at 10K in third at 120 mph is punished by the bike teaching you what it will do in a flurry of pavement, parts, and pain.

Here's another example: You're out on your cruiser and you lean it into a turn and suddenly (and you've hear this) "I leaned, and the bike wouldn't lean any further...I got on the brakes but the thing wouldn't steer, and I wound up in the bushes..." or "I was hot into the turn, and the bike wouldn't make it, so I had to lay it down!" Oh, that bike will make that turn. How do I know? Because, until you're grinding hard parts, the bike will lean further. Once you're grinding, you can hang off if you need to. The problem isn't the bike can't do it. The issue is *you're* just not capable of doing it—you're trying to make the bike submit and instead of squeezing harder, you've decided that you're doing the most you can do, and you quit trying. The bike simply will do more than you can. *Admit it. Accept it.* Then start expanding your boundaries, build yourself into the rider your bike deserves.

During the summer I teach people to ride. I also ride with experienced riders. Both flavors continue to make the same mistake—they try to make the bike submit to their will; they try to dominate the bike and force it to do what they think it should do. We riders buy books and videos that we think will give us some magical skill or move that will break the bike and make it submit so we can bend it to our will. That's a very common mistake we all make. We watch skilled riders, and we want to be like them. We search for training and tips to be like that rider, when we should be working on getting the most out of ourselves and our ride. That classic drive to be better can absolutely break you as a rider, because if you believe that riding is about dominating the bike and submitting it to your will, you are confused. The bike can do what the bike can do, and if you're lucky you can hang with it to ninety percent of its potential. Yeah, almost all those guys and gals who crash and say, "bad tires" or "ran out of lean" or "the bike wouldn't turn" are full of it. The bike could—the rider wouldn't.

Think of it as a horse. Anyone can sit on it. Anyone can kick it in the ribs and get bucked off. Anyone can trot it and maybe even gallop, but to get that horse to do what it is capable of you have to submit to the idea that you might be the weak link, that you may be the part of the equation that is lacking, that you aren't there to make the horse do your bidding—you are there to help the horse perform to the best of its ability.

I was watching some video on the web the other day, and I was saddened by what I saw. It was a scene I've witnessed dozens of times on the range with new riders. A gentleman had gone to the trouble of videotaping himself putting around at speeds less than three miles per hour and then posted it as some kind of odd benchmark used to measure "control." As counter-intuitive as it may be, motorcycles don't like going three miles per hour, they are strikingly unstable at low speeds. Watching the video I saw what I have seen so many times before—new riders desperately trying to control a slow-moving motorcycle. There's twitching and flopping around, and knees pop out, and shoulders snap back and forth like some poor sap caught in the misery of a fevered dream or a seizure.

Motorcycles do not like to go really slow and to pointlessly try and dominate one at ultra-low speeds is painful to watch. In the training world we coach unstable riders to speed up and stabilize the bike. Why? Because a motorcycle stabilizes with speed. To spend your time trying to make a bike do something it doesn't want to do, to try and dominate it and make it submit to you, is foolishness of the first order.

I am not saying that you don't steer and control the bike; I'm saying that you need to accept that the bike has design parameters and set up issues and a thousand little variables that, in the end, determine what it's capable of. If you don't get that, if you keep trying to shove a square peg into a round hole, your riding experience probably won't be what you would like it to be, and eventually something is gonna get broken—you or the bike. By submitting to the bike, searching out its possibilities, and recognizing your own shortcomings you can start being the rider the bike needs. Remember that guy who said the bike "wouldn't turn" and wound up in the ditch? What do you want to bet that bike could make that turn. Why is it that as badly as someone wants to dominate their bike and make it do something, no matter how many DVDs they buy or how long they obsess about the right tire or gloves—why can't they make that bike do what they want it to do? Because, in truth, *they* are the piece that is lacking.

One of the most pitiful things you can hear from a rider is this sad, silly surrender: "My bike won't do that." I have a hard time respecting a rider who blames the bike because the bike *will* do that. The truthful statement would be: "My bike will do that, I'm just not there yet." Yup, your bike will do that, and if you can't...so what? Nitwits like me spend hours honing ourselves so we can do silly things you may never, ever need to do in the real world. Some of that training pays off in the real world and some doesn't—so what? Should you get up every morning, pour yourself a cup of Joe, walk out to your bike, and apologize for not riding to its full potential? Maybe...especially if you spend all your time trying to make it do things that it wants to do, but you don't know how to pull off. Speaking of which; when you ask a bike to pull a boneheaded play, it will. Every bike will wheelie if you're comfortable planting that tach on the red line and dropping the clutch in first gear. I watched a newbie rider do a killer twelve o'clock tail-scraper, complete with feet off the pegs— on a Nighthawk 250. I had a lady lift the front of a low slung Sportster at me from a dead stop; thankfully she grabbed the clutch while I ran for my life. You can ride your bike right, and you can ride your bike wrong, but be in charge of your riding; control your own life. The first step to a better riding career is understanding that the weak link isn't the bike—it is you. Put another rider in the saddle, one who's willing to work with the bike, instead of simply humping its leg, and he will make it do what you say it can't do.

Submitting is not quitting. Submitting is not crying "Uncle." Submitting is giving yourself to the bike in the same way you want it to submit to you; it is being the ideal mate. No one likes to talk about how it takes two to make a great marriage, but both people have to submit to the other, and in the end both are better served as the other watches out for their needs and helps polish their virtues.

Submit yourself to the bike and accept the bike's submission. Be a partner and not a master—things will be great.

Wherever you go, enjoy the journey.

When you can, journey with those you love.

If you travel alone, may you soon enjoy reunion.

May your mechanicals be sound and your tires always full.

And whatever you ride, ride it well.

Be Safe.